Building Basic Skills in Reading

Book 1

Building Basic Skills in Reading

Book 1

CB

CONTEMPORARY BOOKS

a division of NTC/CONTEMPORARY PUBLISHING GROUP
Lincolnwood, Illinois USA

Library of Congress Cataloging-in-Publication Data
Main entry under title:

Building basic skills in reading.

    1. Readers—1950–   2. Reading (Adult education)
3. Reading comprehension.   4. Basic education.
I. Contemporary Books, inc.
PE1126.A4B8   428.6   81-804
ISBN 0-8092-5878-1 (pbk.)

ISBN: 0-8092-5878-1

Published by Contemporary Books,
a division of NTC/Contemporary Publishing Group, Inc.,
4255 West Touhy Avenue,
Lincolnwood (Chicago), Illinois 60646-1975 U.S.A.

1 2 3 C(K) 30 29 28

ACKNOWLEDGMENTS

The thoughtful efforts of a great many people went into the preparation of Contemporary Books' *Building Basic Skills* series. We gratefully acknowledge their contributions and continued involvement in Adult Education.

Adult Education Division

Lillian J. Fleming, Editorial Director
Barbara Drazin, Editor
Wendy Harris, Marketing Services Coordinator

Production Department

Deborah Eisel, Production Editor

Reading and Readability Editors

Jane L. Evanson
Helen B. Ward
Norma Libman

Deborah Nathan
Jane Friedland
Donna Wynbrandt

Authors and Contributors

Writing: Rob Sax

Social Studies: Robert Schambier
Carol Hagel
Phil Smolik
Jack Lesar
Nora Ishibashi
Helen T. Bryant
Jo Ann Kawell
Deborah Brewster
Mary E. Bromage
Sheldon B. Silver
Patricia Miripol

Science: Ronald LeMay
Cynthia Talbert
Jeffrey Miripol
John Gloor
William Collien
Charles Nissim-Sabat

Reading: Timothy A. Foote
Raymond Traynor
Pamela D. Drell (Editor)

Mathematics: Jerry Howett

Project Assistance
Sara Plath

Graphic Art: Louise Hodges
Cover Design: Jeff Barnes

CONTENTS

TO THE LEARNER ix

PRE-TEST 1
   Answers and Explanations—Pre-Test 13
   Pre-Test Skill Mastery Chart 16

1 UNDERSTANDING PARAGRAPHS
   What Is a Paragraph? 17
   Understanding Main Ideas and Supporting Details 21
   Understanding the Main Idea When It Is Stated 23
   Finding the Main Idea When It Is Not Stated Directly .. 25
   Looking for Supporting Details 34
   Remembering Details 44
      Make Mind Pictures and Mind Sounds 45
      Put Yourself in the Situation 46
      Relate to Something You Already Know 50
   Practice Remembering Details 50
   Review Exercises—Understanding Paragraphs 56
   Answers and Explanations—Understanding Paragraphs 68
   Answers and Explanations—Review Exercises 73

2 HOW DETAILS ARE ARRANGED
   Sequences—Time, Place, Ideas and Events 76
      Putting Things in Order by Time 76
      Putting Things in Order by Place 83
      Putting Things in Order by Ideas 86
      Putting Things in Order by Events 88
   Relationships 91
      Seeing Cause and Effect Relationships 91
      Seeing Relationships of Comparison and Contrast .. 94
      Seeing Rank of Importance 98
   Practice 100
   Review Exercises—How Details Are Arranged 104
   Answers and Explanations—How Details Are Arranged 113
   Answers and Explanations—Review Exercises 120

3 LEARNING NEW WORDS WHEN READING

Using Context to Learn New Words 123
Using Synonyms and Antonyms 125
Using Examples and Descriptions 127
Using Word Parts 129
    Root Words 131
    Prefixes 131
    Suffixes 133
Looking at Compound Words 135
Review Exercises—Learning New Words When Reading 140
Answers and Explanations—Learning New Words When Reading . 144
Answers and Explanations—Review Exercises 149

4 MAKING INFERENCES

What Are Inferences? 151
More About Making Inferences 164
Review Exercises—Making Inferences 164
Answers and Explanations—Making Inferences 169
Answers and Explanations—Review Exercises 172

POST-TEST 174

Answers and Explanations—Post-Test 184
Post-Test Skill Mastery Chart 187

TO THE LEARNER

Building Basic Skills in Reading, Books 1 and 2 will give you, the learner, all you need to master the basics of reading well. Together, the books give a complete program that is easy to use on your own or with a teacher in class. The following chart shows the reading skills covered in each book.

BUILDING BASIC SKILLS IN READING	
Book 1	Book 2

Understanding Paragraphs
  Main Idea: Stated and
   Unstated
  Supporting Details
 	
How Details Are Arranged
  Sequence
  Relationships
   Cause and Effect
   Comparison and
    Contrast
   Rank of Importance
 	
Learning New Words When
  Reading
   Context
   Synonyms and Antonyms
   Examples and Descriptions
   Root Words, Prefixes and
    Suffixes
   Compound Words
 	
Making Inferences
	Critical Reading
	  Facts and Opinions
	  Bias
	  Propaganda
	  Style and Tone
	
	Practical Reading—Following
	  Written Directions
	
	Practical Reading—Charts and
	  Illustrations
	   Diagrams
	   Charts
	   Listings and Schedules
	   Graphs

HOW TO USE THIS BOOK

Each unit of *Building Basic Skills in Reading* has plenty of exercises to give you practice in the reading skills covered. The exercises have questions for you to answer. All answers are in the answer section at the end of each unit. You will be able to check your work quickly and easily using this section.

Each unit also ends with a few Review Exercises. These Review Exercises will cover all the new ideas presented in the unit.

Before you begin working, you should start with the **Pre-Test.** This test will show you how much you already know about the skills that are covered in the book. Don't expect to get every answer right on the Pre-Test. If you do, there's no reason for you to read this book! After you take the Pre-Test fill in the Skill Mastery Chart on page 16.

At the very end of the book there is a **Post-Test** which has questions from all of the units. If you understand the units, you should do very well on this test. After you take the Post-Test, fill in the Skill Mastery Chart on page 187. By that time you will be able to look at how you did on both the Pre- and Post-Tests. This will show how much stronger your reading skills have become.

WHY ARE READING SKILLS IMPORTANT?

Reading is one of the most important skills a person can have in life. Being a good reader makes getting and keeping a good job easier. Having good reading skills makes learning about new things much easier. You can get through life not being able to read, but many things are easier if you can read well.

There are many reading skills. Part of reading is knowing what words look like written down and being able to figure out new words. But reading also means sorting out what you have read and understanding what the writer's purpose is. A lot of reading is thinking about the words on the page. That is hard unless you can easily understand them.

The work in *Building Basic Skills in Reading* is meant to be fun and interesting as well as helpful. The examples, exercises, reviews and tests will build your basic reading skills and pave the way for you to go on to higher levels of reading and learning. We hope you enjoy your work.

The Editors of Contemporary Books

PRE-TEST

Directions: The purpose of the Pre-Test is to show you the kind of work you will be doing in *Building Basic Skills in Reading, Book 1*. It will also give you an idea of how much you already know about the skills that will be covered.

The Pre-Test has a total of 33 questions. There is no time limit for the test. You can take a break while you're working on it. When you're done, check your answers on page 13. Then fill in the Skill Mastery Chart on page 16.

On Thanksgiving Eve five years ago Fritz Kooger, a short bald man, got on a jet going from Los Angeles to San Francisco. He carried a small bag with him and took a seat next to the aisle.

A half hour after the jet had taken off, Fritz Kooger rose from his seat. He walked to the rear of the plane, his bag in his hand.

He cornered a stewardess in the rear and said, "I've got a bomb in this bag and a gun in my pocket. Take me to the pilot!"

Fritz followed the stewardess up front to the cockpit. He told the pilot, "Radio to Seattle. Talk to the International Airways office there. I want $300,000 in cash and a parachute. Skip San Francisco and land at Seattle for the cash and chute. Any funny business and we all die." Then, he went back to the cabin and sat in a front seat.

The pilot announced to the passengers, "Because of events beyond our control, we will land in Seattle instead of

San Francisco. We will arrive in Seattle in half an hour. Sorry to inconvenience you."

The jet landed in Seattle. Fritz let all the passengers off, but made the crew stay on.

A man from International Airways brought two bags on to the plane. One held the money, the other held the parachute.

At the rear of the plane Fritz counted the money and transferred it to a money belt. He strapped this around his waist. He dressed himself in a thermal jump suit and ordered the pilot to take off for San Francisco.

At a spot over the mountains of Oregon, Fritz donned his parachute. He opened an emergency door and jumped into 25-degree-below-zero weather. That was the last anyone ever saw of Fritz Kooger.

None of the marked money has ever been found. The following summer two hikers found a rotting jump suit and parts of a parachute in the Oregon mountains. But there is still no trace of Fritz Kooger.

Below is a list of places. Following this list are some events from the story. After each event, write in the name of the place where the event happened. Some places may be used more than once.

in Los Angeles   from the cockpit of the jet
in San Francisco   in the Oregon mountains
in Seattle   at the rear of the jet

1. Fritz boards the jetliner _____

2. Kooger threatens the stewardess with gun and bomb

   _____

3. The jet was originally supposed to land _____

4. Kooger contacted the Airways office to give his demands _____

5. The money and parachute were brought on the jet___

_____

6. Kooger let all the passengers off the plane _____

_____

7. Kooger counted the money and put on his parachute

_____

8. Kooger jumped from the plane _____

_____

9. International Airways had their offices _____

_____

10. A rotting jump suit and parachute were found _____

_____

_____

In each exercise there is an underlined compound word. Each compound word is made up of two words. In the blanks write down the first part of the compound word, the second part of the compound word and what you think the whole word means.

11. The sidewinder is called that because of the odd way this snake crawls through the desert.

1st Part: _____

2nd Part:_____

Meaning: _____

_____

12. Nothing was decided by the game. It ended in a deadlock.

1st Part: _____

2nd Part: _____

Meaning: _____

_____

13. Bonnie wanted the evening to last <u>forever.</u> She knew, though, that it would have to end.

1st Part: _____

2nd Part:_____

Meaning: _____

14. It was <u>foolhardy</u> for the girl to run into the burning house just to save a cat.

1st Part: _____

2nd Part:_____

Meaning: _____

_____

15. Jim won't give up any of his old ideas. He's what you call a real <u>diehard.</u>

1st Part: _____

2nd Part:_____

Meaning: _____

_____

_____

Read this story. Then answer the questions that follow.

Young Indian warriors used to eat the hearts of an animal called the fisher. The fisher is a tough and brave animal. Eating fisher hearts would make young warriors brave too. At least the Indian warriors thought so.

The fisher belongs to the same family as the weasel. It grows to about the size of a long dog—the dachshund. Its heavy black fur makes expensive coats.

At one time fisher furs sold for $200 a piece. This almost caused the fisher to be wiped out. Trappers really went after furs worth that much. Now laws protect the fisher, so the animal is still alive.

The fisher moves like a bullet. It runs like a black streak when it's after food. It will even attack and kill another animal like the porcupine. No other animal will touch a porcupine because of its sharp quills. But the fisher eats the porcupine, quills and all. Scientists have found quills in fishers' stomachs and muscles. They have never found any sign of harm from these quills.

When angry, the fisher arches its back like a cat. It hisses and shows a set of sharp, frightening teeth. Its speed and its teeth allow it to win many battles. It can beat animals three times its size.

The fisher is so tough it can't get along even with other fishers. The male stays with the female for only two weeks. The female drives her young ones away from her very soon after they are born.

The male fisher stays alone. He guards his own area in the forest from all comers, including other fishers. He's brave, but he isn't well liked.

16. Put a check in front of the sentence that gives the main idea of the story.

_____(1) Indian warriors ate the hearts of fishers to become brave.

_____(2) The fisher was almost wiped out by trappers at one time.

_____(3) The fisher is a brave and tough animal who isn't very well liked.

_____(4) The fisher is the only animal who will attack and kill a porcupine.

_____(5) none of the above

17.   Fill in the blanks with the correct words from the story.

The fisher grows to be about the size of a _____ . Its heavy _____ makes
(a)   (b)
excellent _____ . At one time they
(c)
were worth _____ . Laws now protect
(d)
the fisher from _____ .
(e)

The fisher is as fast as a bullet and will
attack even a _____ for food. Scien-
(f)
tists have found _____ in fishers'
(g)
stomachs and muscles. But these don't
_____ the fisher.
(h)

When it is angry, the fisher arches its
_____ like a _____ . The fisher
(i)   (j)
is very _____ , but it's not very
(k)
_____ by anyone in the forest.
(l)

Read the passage. Answer the questions that follow it.

Dizzy Dean's given name was Jay Hanna Dean. Back in Arkansas, when Dizzy was a boy, a friend of his died. The friend's name was Jerome Herman. The six-year-old Dizzy felt very sorry for Jerome's father.

Dizzy changed his name from Jay Hanna Dean to Jerome Herman Dean in honor of the dead boy. He told the father, "I'll make Jerome Herman mean something in this world."

Dizzy started school that year. "I went two grades," he said. "The first was harder than the second, so I quit."

The whole Dean family loved baseball. After their farmwork was done, they played catch. Dizzy could hit a snake in the head at 40 paces.

A baseball scout saw Dizzy one day and hired him. He paid Dizzy for playing ball. Dizzy said, "That was the first time I knew you could get paid for playing."

Dizzy turned professional. In his first game as a pitcher, he walked up to each batter and said hello. He asked what kind of pitch the batter wanted him to throw. When the game started, he blazed the ball past each batter.

Another time, he walked up to the other team before the game. He said, "Don't you guys worry about curve balls today. Ole Diz is going to throw just fast balls."

He kept his word. The other team didn't score even one run.

Another time in Cincinnati, Dizzy brought a cake of ice onto the field. He set it on home plate. Someone asked him why. "I want to cool it off from my fast balls," he answered.

Someone said that Dizzy bragged all the time. Dizzy didn't agree. "The way I look at it, bragging is when you can't back it up with any action."

18. What did you find out about the following things that show that Dizzy Dean was an unusual person?

 (a) His name as a child: _____

 _____

 (b) His education: _____

 _____

 (c) What he could do with a baseball on the farm: ___

 _____

 (d) What he found out about pay: _____

 _____

 (e) First game as a professional pitcher: _____

 _____

 (f) Dizzy and the cake of ice: _____

 _____

 (g) Dizzy and bragging: _____

 _____

19.   The main idea about Dizzy Dean is

_____(1)   He changed his name from Jay Hanna to Dizzy Dean.

_____(2)   He never finished school or went to college.

_____(3)   He was a great pitcher and did many unusual things in his life.

_____(4)   He could hit a snake in the head at 40 paces.

_____(5)   He was a good baseball player but he bragged.

_____

Figure out the meaning of the underlined word in each paragraph from its context. Write the meaning of the word in the blank that follows the paragraph.

20.   You're supposed to pour this package of dry powdered milk into the cold water. Make sure you have exactly one quart of water. Add any more than that and you'll <u>dilute</u> the milk too much. It will taste like a weak, white water instead of milk.
Dilute: _____

21.   For children Christmas is a time of <u>anticipation</u>. The big event is Santa Claus' visit and the gifts he will leave on Christmas Eve. Time drags for the kids. What will Santa leave them? Will they get what they ask for? The anticipation is almost more than they can take.
Anticipation: _____

22. The car drove down the street. You could see heavy black smoke pouring from the exhaust pipe. In the city several thousand cars did this every time they started up. No wonder the air of the city is very polluted and hard to breathe.

Polluted: _____

Read the following short story. Answer the questions that follow it.

Two elderly women parked their electric golf cart on the golf course. They walked a few feet away to take their next shots.

Quickly two men jumped out from the trees and ran to the cart. They hopped in and drove away from the women.

The two women chased them, yelling and waving golf clubs. But it was no use. The cart and the men were gone.

Police in almost every good-sized city in America can report strange thefts like this one.

In Los Angeles a young man stole a Greyhound bus and drove it on the highway. He ended up in a town 60 miles away.

His excuse for stealing the bus? He needed a ride but didn't have enough money for the fare. He even picked up passengers along the way and gave them free rides.

All kinds of strange things are stolen. Some thieves like to take things from the city streets. They have stolen manhole covers, street and traffic signs and even parking meters—not just the money in the meter, but the whole thing.

Recently the owner of a barbershop lost a red and white striped barber pole. The pole was 40 years old and was worth $500. The pole weighed more than 260 pounds and was sitting on an iron stand. This stand was bolted to the sidewalk. It must have taken two men several hours to get it loose.

Something can weigh a ton. It can be bolted down. It can be worth very little money. Still someone will come along and steal it.

Put a check mark in front of the best ending for each sentence.

23. Two elderly women
   _____(1)   had their golf clubs stolen.
   _____(2)   were very angry because their game was rained out.
   _____(3)   had their golf cart stolen.
   _____(4)   chased the two men down the street.
   _____(5)   caught the men who stopped their game.

24. Police have reported thefts
   _____(1)   that are very strange.
   _____(2)   that are only annoying.
   _____(3)   that cost the taxpayers millions of dollars.
   _____(4)   that are never really solved.
   _____(5)   that happen only in cities.

25. In Los Angeles one young man stole
   _____(1)   a barber pole.
   _____(2)   several parking meters.
   _____(3)   a golf cart from two elderly women.
   _____(4)   a Greyhound bus.
   _____(5)   all of the above.

26. Big city thieves will even steal things like
   _____(1)   street lights.
   _____(2)   garbage trucks.
   _____(3)   manhole covers.

_____(4) police cars.

_____(5) golf clubs.

27. The stolen barber pole was

_____(1) striped red and blue.

_____(2) striped red and white.

_____(3) striped blue and white.

_____(4) striped black and blue.

_____(5) striped red, white and blue.

28. The barber pole was worth

_____(1) $500.

_____(2) $300.

_____(3) $600.

_____(4) $200.

_____(5) $400.

29. The barber pole was hard to steal because of its

_____(1) weight and age.

_____(2) age and the difficulty in moving it.

_____(3) weight and height.

_____(4) size and color.

_____(5) none of the above

30. The main idea of this passage is that

_____(1) thieves like to steal things from city streets and golf courses.

_____(2) in spite of weight, size or difficulty in moving an object, nothing is safe from thieves.

_____(3) people steal strange things to get their pictures in the newspaper.

_____(4) police can report stories of all the strange things that have been stolen.

_____(5) thieves are more likely to steal something that costs a lot.

Read what was said between two women. Use the facts to make good inferences. Answer the questions that follow.

Claudia: Oh, what are you going to do?

Sylvia: If I can't get a job, I'll have to get on welfare.

Claudia: What kind of job will you look for?

Sylvia: I never worked. I don't know what I can do. And I sure as hell can't feed that man's four children washing dishes. Man! Hah! He's no man after what he did.

Claudia: Sylvia—maybe he'll think of coming back.

Sylvia: That fool can't even think. Let alone think of coming back.

Claudia: But all men go through changes sometimes.

Sylvia: Well, one change he's not going through is from her bed back to mine.

31. Who is the man Claudia and Sylvia are talking about?

_____

_____

32. What must Sylvia have told Claudia just before the conversation you read?

_____

_____

33. How does Sylvia feel as she is talking to Claudia? What is her main emotion?

_____

_____

ANSWERS AND EXPLANATIONS—PRE-TEST

1. Fritz boards the jetliner in Los Angeles.

2. Kooger threatens the stewardess with gun and bomb at the rear of the jet.

3. The jet was originally supposed to land in San Francisco.

4. Kooger contacted the Airways office to give his demands from the cockpit of the jet.

5. The money and parachute were brought on the jet in Seattle.

6. Kooger let all the passengers off the plane in Seattle.

7. Kooger counted the money and put on his parachute at the rear of the jet.

8. Kooger jumped from the plane in the Oregon Mountains.

9. International Airways had their offices in Seattle.

10. A rotting jump suit and parachute were found in the Oregon mountains.

11. side winder—it crawls to the side instead of going straight ahead.
12. dead lock—neither side won; a tie.
13. for ever—not ending; going on and on.
14. fool hardy—bold but foolish.
15. die hard—won't give up; sticks to the same ideas right to the end; stubborn.

16. (3) is the only one that states the author's main idea. If you look at the beginning of the story you'll see the main idea there. Also, the main idea is written again at the end of the story.

17. In some of these, your answers may be slightly different.

The fisher grows to be about the size of a <u>dachshund (or long dog)</u>. Its heavy <u>fur</u> makes excellent (a)   (b)
<u>coats</u>. At one time they were worth <u>$200.</u> Laws now (c)   (d)
protect the fisher from <u>trappers</u>. (e)

The fisher is as fast as a bullet and will attack even a <u>porcupine</u> for food. Scientists have found (f)
<u>porcupine quills</u> in fishers' stomachs and muscles. But (g)
these don't <u>bother (harm or hurt)</u> the fisher. (h)

When it is angry, the fisher arches its <u>back</u> like a (i)
<u>cat</u>. The fisher is very <u>tough</u>, but it's not very <u>well</u> (j)   (k)   (l)
<u>liked</u> by anyone in the forest.

---

18. Make sure your answers have the correct ideas. Your words may be slightly different.

(a) The first thing the author tells about Dizzy Dean is how and why he changed his name. He changed it in honor of a friend who died. He did this as a child.

(b) Dizzy made a joke about his education by saying he quit after the second grade. This is the second unusual thing about Dizzy.

(c) A third unusual thing about Dizzy was his skill at throwing. At 40 paces he could hit a snake in the head.

(d) A scout discovered Dizzy and hired him to play baseball. Dizzy had never heard of playing for money.

(e) Another thing Dizzy did in his first professional game was to go up to each batter and say hello. He asked what kind of pitch each batter wanted.

(f) In one game he put a cake of ice on home plate to cool it off from his fast balls.

(g) Dizzy believed it wasn't bragging if you could do what you said.

19. (3) is the correct answer. You can see that the author shows Dizzy was an unusual person. The main idea is that Dizzy Dean was a great baseball pitcher who did many unusual things in his life.

20. Dilute: to make something weaker by mixing another thing into it; to water something down

21. Anticipation: eagerly waiting for; looking forward to

22. Polluted: filled with harmful things; dirty or impure

23. (3) had their golf cart stolen by two men.

24. (1) The story is about strange things people steal.

25. (4) The man stole a Greyhound bus in Los Angeles.

26. (3) Manhole covers are one of the strange things some thieves will take.

27. (2) The owner of a barbershop lost a red and white striped barber pole.

28. (1) The pole was more than 40 years old and worth $500.

29. (5) It wasn't any of these. It was the fact that it was bolted to the cement sidewalk.

30. (2) Nothing is safe. Thieves will steal all sorts of strange things in spite of their size or how difficult they would be to move.

31. Sylvia's husband. Or, the father of Sylvia's children.

32. She must have just told Claudia that her husband (or children's father) had walked out on her. Also, that he left her for another woman.

33. She is very angry. You can feel the anger in the last three things Sylvia says.

PRE-TEST SKILL MASTERY CHART

Directions: Fill in the Skill Mastery Chart after you have checked your answers on the Pre-Test. Each skill on the test is listed with the test questions using that skill. Circle each question you answered correctly. Then count your total number of circled answers and write this in the box under Number Correct. Next, find the Skill Mastery Level that fits your number correct. Place a check (✔) in the box at the correct level. Do this for each skill listed. Then find your total number of correct answers and total number of checks at each Skill Mastery Level. The Skill Mastery Chart will tell you which skills you should work with most in this book.

SKILL	TOTAL SCORE	NUMBER CORRECT	SKILL MASTERY LEVELS			STUDY PAGES
			SKILL MASTERY	PRACTICE & REVIEW NEEDED	FULL LEARNING NEEDED	
			(Check one box in each row)			
1 Seeing the Main Idea and Supporting Details 16, 17, 18, 19, 23, 24, 25, 26, 27, 28, 29, 30	12		12-9	8-5	4-0	17-75
2 How Details Are Arranged-Sequence 1, 2, 3, 4, 5 6, 7, 8, 9, 10	10		10-8	7-5	4-0	76-122
3 Learning New Words When Reading 11, 12, 13, 14, 15 20, 21, 22	8		8-7	6-4	3-0	123-150
4 Making Inferences 31, 32, 33	3		3-2	1	0	151-173
TOTAL	33					

1 UNDERSTANDING PARAGRAPHS

Let's begin with paragraphs and how to read them. In this unit we will talk about how to find the main idea of a paragraph and about how writers use details to support their main ideas. We will also see that stories are built from groups of paragraphs and that stories, too, have a main idea and supporting details.

WHAT IS A PARAGRAPH?

Sometimes when you talk you want to pass along some news or information. Other times there is a different reason for talking. For example, saying "Hi" or "What's happening!" is just a friendly greeting. Saying those things is not meant to pass on news.

The sentences that follow pass along some information:

> My mother just went into the hospital the other day. She's going blind. She has never been good about taking her diabetes medicine. Under a doctor's care I hope she'll do much better.

If someone says all that to you, you know something you didn't know before. You have new information. It came across in the statements about the person's mother. When information comes across, there has to be a topic. What is the news about? That is the topic. Look back at the above sentences. What is each and every sentence about? Each one is about the person's mother. She is the topic or subject of all the sentences.

A **paragraph**, then, is a group of sentences that all have the same topic. Suppose you say:

> Willie got arrested today for drunk driving. My cat had fleas last year. When will Sandra get married? My mother loves me and my sister. Then we'll have time to eat a good breakfast.

This is **not** a paragraph. All these sentences have different topics.

It is an easy step from here to see that stories, articles and passages are made of a set of paragraphs. Each paragraph talks about a part of the main topic of the story, article or passage. For now, let's go back to single paragraphs. Later in this unit you will work with groups of paragraphs in stories.

Read the paragraph below. Then write down its topic.

> "I use it for everything, even slicing garlic. You think it's too big for that? Well, let me tell you, this cleaver has been the only knife I've used in my kitchen for four years. I've never had to sharpen it, either. I wouldn't trade it in for anything."
>
> Topic: _____

The topic of this paragraph is "my (his, her, the) cleaver," or "my (his, her, the) knife." Every sentence is about the knife.

Read the following two paragraphs. In the space after each paragraph write down in a few words what the topic of the paragraph is.

The Equal Rights Amendment (ERA) has one main purpose. That purpose is to make sure that women have a status which, by law, is equal to men's—in every way. Some who argue against the ERA try to scare women. They say, "Then you'll be drafted and have to go to war if we get into one."

Topic: _____

Who says clothes don't make the man? Nathaniel Hawthorne wrote a story about a Christian minister. That man wore a black cloth in front of his face until he died. People were afraid of him because of the veil. But they came to him with their problems because they thought he had power. Both their fear and their idea that he had power came from the black cloth. It was a different piece of clothing. It made him a unique man.

Topic: _____

The topic of the first paragraph is the Equal Rights Amendment (ERA). Even the part about women being drafted is related to the topic, the ERA.

There are a few choices for the topic of the second paragraph. Any of these will do:

(a) the black cloth (or veil)
(b) the minister's black cloth (or veil)
(c) clothes make the man

The sentences are not about Nathaniel Hawthorne, men and their clothing, what people thought about the minister or even about the minister. The <u>veil</u> is the thing discussed.   It is the topic.

After you name the topic of a paragraph, there is only one more step to stating the main idea. To find a main idea you first name the topic and then ask, <u>"What do I know about that?"</u>

Read this paragraph. The topic is blackouts. Complete the sentence following the paragraph with a short statement about blackouts.

If a person "blacks out" when drinking, it is not that he passes out. What this really means is that when the person sobers up, he will not remember anything that happened after the blackout. A person can be drinking with friends and black out. The person's behavior may not change at all. He may not know he blacked out. But in the morning, the person will not remember what happened after he blacked out. The blackout is a memory loss or blocking, not a fainting.

Blackouts are _____

_____

A good answer would be: "Blackouts are losses of memory caused by drinking." Or just: "Blackouts are losses of memory." It would not be as good to say: "Blackouts are not faintings." That just tells you what they <u>are</u> <u>not</u>, not what they <u>are</u>.

The main idea of a paragraph, then, is made up of two things:

(1) the topic

(2) a statement about the topic.

When paragraphs make up a story, you will be able to find the story's main idea in the same way: There will be a topic. After reading the story or passage, you will also know something about the story's topic.

UNDERSTANDING MAIN IDEAS AND SUPPORTING DETAILS

You might ask: Why don't writers give us only their main idea? Why don't they just forget all the added details? To see why writers don't do this, read this main idea:

As a kid, I was always afraid of walking past the corner of Elm and 52nd Street because of what happened there.

Doesn't the main idea alone leave some questions in your mind? You probably feel left up in the air.

In the following blanks write three questions you might want the writer to answer about this corner.

1. _____

_____

2. _____

_____

3. _____

_____

Some of the questions you might want the author to answer are these: Why is the writer afraid of this corner? Where is the corner anyway? What's on the corner of Elm and 52nd Street? Did some terrible accident happen to the writer there? Did someone attack or mug him?

You probably could think of many more questions. Perhaps by now you are interested in finding out about the corner. So let's add some details to fill in the story.

As a kid I was always afraid of walking past the corner of Elm and 52nd Street. I used to go nearly a half mile out of my way to avoid it.

This corner was a vacant lot with tall weeds and bushes. My brother and I had to walk by the corner on our way to St. Jude's School.

Sometimes, a gang called the "Butchers" waited for us in the weeds. Just as we got to the corner, they all jumped out. They started after us throwing dirt clods.

Naturally we ran. One day I turned to see if they were really chasing us. A clod caught me in the mouth. My two front teeth were knocked out and blood gushed from my mouth. . . .

At this point in the story, many of our questions have been answered. We've found out something that tells us why the writer was so afraid of this corner.

Supporting details answer many of the questions we would have about an idea if the idea were simply stated by itself. The details are facts which give us examples and clearer pictures of the main idea.

UNDERSTANDING THE MAIN IDEA WHEN IT IS STATED

Remember how the story about the corner of Elm and 52nd Street began. This was the first paragraph:

> As a kid I was always afraid of walking past the corner of Elm and 52nd Street. I used to go nearly a half mile out of my way to avoid it.

This first paragraph has the main idea of the whole story right in it. The writer stated his main idea directly. It was the first sentence of the story. But the main idea doesn't have to be at the beginning of a paragraph or a story. It might come anywhere. It might also be stated in more than one place or in more than one sentence.

Exercise 1

In each of the paragraphs below, the main idea is stated directly. Each sentence in each paragraph is numbered. In the blanks after each paragraph, write what you think is the topic of the paragraph. Then write what you learn about the topic (the main idea). Finally, write the number of the sentence in the paragraph that states the main idea. Check your answers.

(1) "The drinks cost $3.00, and there's hardly any liquor in them. (2) To get in the door, you have to pay a $2.00 cover. (3) You don't get anything for that, but 'in.' (4) That's at Frisco's. (5) That new disco is too expensive for me." (6) "They named it the right thing! (7) They 'frisco' you and take all your money."

1. Topic: _____

    Main Idea: _____

    Number of sentence which states main idea: _____

    _____

(1) Cable has improved television reception. (2) Areas in large cities often have poor reception. (3) Either the picture or the sound is poor, or both are. (4) Sometimes it is impossible to get certain channels. (5) These problems are often due to nearby tall buildings. (6) The buildings block TV signals. (7) With cable, programs come through wire. (8) The signal cannot be blocked. (9) Every channel is clear and bright. (10) With cable, it is possible to get more channels than without cable.

2. Topic: _____

    Main Idea: _____

    Number of sentence which states main idea: _____

    _____

(1) The dogs called shepherds are known for many things. (2) One is that they love to lick people's feet. (3) Through the centuries, shepherds have had that habit bred into them. (4) They have been good company for men who walk all day. (5) Those men raised and taught generations of shepherds to lick their feet. (6) Probably there is nothing more relaxing in the world. (7) Now, by instinct, shepherds lick people's feet to help the people relax.

3. Topic: _____

    Main Idea: _____

    Number of sentence which states main idea: _____

    _____

(1) How did the use of "OK" begin? (2) Americans are known around the world for saying, "OK." (3) No one seems to know just where it came from. (4) One idea is that President Theodore Roosevelt started the use of "OK." (5)

It is said that Roosevelt couldn't spell very well. (6) When he wanted to give something his approval, he wrote, "Ol Kerect!" (7) He meant, "All correct!" (8) The initials of what he wrote are "O.K." (9) Maybe that's how it was!

4.   Topic: _____

Main Idea: _____

Number of sentence which states main idea: _____

Answers start on page 68.

FINDING THE MAIN IDEA WHEN IT IS NOT STATED DIRECTLY

Many times writers don't put down their main ideas in words. They tell their story. You, the reader, must then figure out what their main ideas are.

Suppose the writer of the corner story didn't want to state his main idea directly. He could write the story like this:

> There was on empty lot on the corner of Elm and 52nd Street filled with tall weeds and bushes. My brother and I had to pass it each day. We were on our way to St. Jude's School.
>
> One morning as we walked by, a gang called the "Butchers" was hiding in the weeds. As we passed, they jumped up and threw dirt clods at us.
>
> Naturally, we ran. I turned to see if they were really chasing us. A clod caught me in the mouth. I felt blood pouring from my mouth.
>
> After this we went six blocks out of our way to avoid the "Butchers" at Elm and 52nd Street. That was their territory.

You can see how the writer hasn't directly stated his main idea. He's told us the details of the story. We can figure out the main idea for ourselves.

Here is another short story. It has no main idea directly stated by the writer. Read it. See if you, the reader, can state the main idea. Write this idea in the blank after the story. Remember, the main idea is the topic and what you learn about the topic.

We were very hungry. The sign in the window read, "Joe's Coffee Shop." Almost all the paint on the sign was faded.

We could hardly see through the glass. At first we thought the window was just steamed over. But the steam turned out to be grease.

When we opened the door, the odor of old hamburger meat almost knocked us back. But we went and sat down at the counter. Flies buzzed around us.

One customer sat at the counter talking to the cook. The cook had on a dirty apron and a grease-covered hat. He threw his cigarette on the floor and stepped on it. He grunted at us, "What are you guys going to have?"

My friend Jim replied, "Oh, I'm not very hungry. I'll just have a bottle of root beer."

At least a bottle of pop would be clean. So I said, "I'll take one too."

Main Idea: _____

_____

_____

For the main idea you could say something like this. "The two people were very hungry, but the coffee shop was too dirty to eat in." Or, "The two people lost their appetites in this dirty, greasy coffee shop." Your words don't have to be exactly the same as these, but by asking yourself what the topic is and what you know about it, you should have come up with the same idea.

Exercise 2

Read the following story and answer the questions after them. Then check your answers.

Mistake Number One

It was quitting time. Debbie Muffet was very excited. She hurried from the New Town Cafe where she was a waitress. She was rushing to buy her first car.

Jim Lott, a cook at the New Town, had just sold his 1977 Datsun with 80,000 miles on it to Debbie. Debbie took the bus to Lott's apartment.

She gave Lott a check for $850, all the money she had in the bank. She drove the car from Lott's place. She headed across town to her friend Alice's apartment. She'd promised Alice a ride in the car.

They took the freeway to Porterville. On the way out the car sounded very good. But on the trip back they heard a big clunk under the hood.

Debbie pulled to the curb. The two girls climbed out. They couldn't tell what was wrong. The car just wouldn't move.

Debbie called Lott and asked him to come and look. "Remember," Lott said, "you bought the car as is. Anything that goes wrong is your problem."

The transmission was shot. It would cost at least $500 for a new one.

Debbie called a nearby gas station to tow the car in. That cost $25 by itself. Debbie didn't have the money to fix the car. She'd have to find a way to borrow it.

She was angry with Lott. How could he have left her with a worn out car? During all this, Debbie lost a friend, $850 for the car and $500 for repairs. She had made a big mistake.

1. Put a check mark in front of the sentence that best states the main idea.

    _____(1)   It is very foolish to buy used cars because they fall apart.

    _____(2)   Women should never buy used cars from men.

    _____(3)   You should never drive a used car on the freeway.

    _____(4)   You shouldn't buy a used car unless you have extra money to fix it.

    _____(5)   Buying used cars from friends is a gamble because there is no warranty on them.

2. Which of the following statements are true? Write T in front of those that are true. Write F in front of those that are false.

    _____(a)   Lott dumped his worn out car on Debbie.

    _____(b)   The transmission on the car went out on the first trip.

    _____(c)   Debbie paid less than $750 for Lott's car.

    _____(d)   Both Lott and Debbie worked at the New Town Cafe.

    _____(e)   Debbie paid $100 just to tow the car into the garage.

Answers start on page 68.

Exercise 3

Mistake Number Two

Eric Redmon had been looking at the shiny auto every day. It was a sharp 1978 Pontiac LeMans. It sat on the front row of Honest Al's Used Car Lot.

Eric had saved $200 from working as a bag boy at Johnson's Supermarket. Honest Al wanted $950 for the Pontiac. He told Eric to put the $200 down. Then Al would loan Eric $750 at regular interest rates.

Each day Honest Al pushed Eric. "Hey, kid, you better put the $200 down on the Pontiac today. Somebody'll grab that car. It's a sharp one."

Jack Barter, the bookkeeper at Johnson's, warned Eric, "Stay away from fly-by-night guys like Honest Al. He buys cars that no one else wants. You could easily get stuck with a lemon."

Jack also said, "Buy from a dealer who also sells new cars. He'll stand behind the cars he sells. And he'll have a repair shop too. Watch out if Honest Al wants to loan you money. He could take you real bad."

The next day Eric passed Honest Al's and saw a guy looking at the Pontiac. He rushed home and got his $200. He bought the Pontiac.

Eric drove the car for 300 miles. It burned oil. It needed motor work. The sales slip said the car was sold "as is." Eric was stuck with a big repair bill right away. He couldn't use the car. But his payments went on anyway. Eric learned a good lesson about buying used cars.

1. Complete this sentence about the main idea of this story. You are taking a gamble if you buy a car

2. Pick the word or phrase from the second column that fits with the word or phrase in the first. Write the letter in the blank.

_____1. Pontiac LeMans	(a)	a bookkeeper
_____2. Jack Barter	(b)	a used car lot
_____3. $200	(c)	a bag boy
_____4. $750	(d)	those bought by Honest Al
_____5. Eric's job	(e)	1978 used car
_____6. "as is" condition	(f)	Eric's down payment
_____7. cars that nobody else wanted	(g)	in present condition with no guarantee
_____8. Honest Al's	(h)	Eric's loan

Answers start on page 69.

Exercise 4

Exercise 4 and 5 give two different sides of the same story. Read each story and answer the questions.

Teenage Marriage—Laura's Side

I met Bill when we were sophomores in high school. After a few dates we fell in love. Bill was tall and good looking. He was the first boy I was ever serious about. I really liked being with him.

That spring I got pregnant. Bill did the honorable thing. We got married. Right away my family put me out.

We both quit school. Bill got a job at a gas station for $3 an hour. We found a real small apartment for $100 a month. I worked at the dime store for a while.

At first we were looking forward to the baby. Bill wanted a boy.

After six months I had to quit my job. Then I had trouble delivering the baby. It cost us nearly $4,000. With food, rent, car payments and the hospital bills, we couldn't make ends meet.

Bill started acting nasty and staying out late at night. He argued over everything all the time. I gained 40 pounds. He started calling me "Fats."

The finance company took back our car. The landlord was about to throw us out for not paying the rent.

One night after a real bad fight I packed up. I took the baby and moved in with my sister. I filed for a divorce.

Bill quit his job. He moved to Las Vegas. He doesn't send me any money. So I'm on welfare, and I get food stamps.

It's hard for me to work with the baby being so young. Besides that, I have no skills, not even a high school diploma. Now my sister's getting tired of us too. I sure wish I had it to do over again.

1. Laura tells a sad story here about her experience. Ask yourself this: What is she trying to say? In other words, what is her main idea?

   Write it here: _____

   _____

   _____

2. What caused the trouble? Read the following details that support the story's main idea. Put yes in front of the ones you think caused the break-up of Laura's marriage. Write no in front of those you don't think were important in causing trouble. Write maybe in

front of those that you think may be true but are not really backed up by facts in the story.

_____(a)   Laura and Bill fell in love.

_____(b)   They were sophomores in high school at the time.

_____(c)   Laura became pregnant though they weren't married.

_____(d)   Both of them quit school right away.

_____(e)   Neither of them seemed to have any job skills.

_____(f)   Bill married Laura because he wanted to do the "honorable" thing.

_____(g)   At first Laura and Bill looked forward to having their baby.

_____(h)   Laura had to quit her job to have the baby.

_____(i)   The cost of having the baby came to nearly $4,000.

_____(j)   Laura gained 40 pounds after having the baby.

Answers start on page 69.

Exercise 5

Teenage Marriage—Bill's Side

Look at her now—sloppy and fat. Laura wasn't that way when we were going together. She had a sharp figure.

She got pregnant, and we were married. Then she started letting everything go. She didn't know how to cook, couldn't even boil water. And she didn't care.

Before the baby came, she was still working. We ate a lot of TV dinners and junk food. Laura was also a lousy housekeeper. There were always dishes in the sink and dirty clothes all over. Papers and garbage were everywhere. I couldn't stand that for long.

When the baby came home, things were worse. The baby cost us $4,000. Laura was always yelling and complaining. Three or four times we had some real battles. Finally, I couldn't take it anymore, so I moved out.

I know I haven't sent her any money. But how can I? I have to spend all I make just to live here in Las Vegas. Working in a gas station doesn't give you much money.

I'm trying to go to night school and get my diploma. I want to learn to be a mechanic when I get some money saved and some time. Then I can send Laura and the kid some money. But she ought to get up and work too.

She needs to lose weight and take care of herself. She needs to set some goals like I have. No, I'll never make up with her. She had her chance with me and messed it all up.

1. Write the main idea of Bill's side here:_____

_____

_____

_____

2. Use the supporting details of Bill's side of the story. Write <u>yes</u> in front of the following sentences if they are true. Write <u>no</u> in front of the ones that are not true.

Bill blames Laura for:
_____(a) getting pregnant.
_____(b) being a very poor cook.
_____(c) having a messy apartment.
_____(d) letting her looks go.
_____(e) quitting high school before she learned a skill.
_____(f) failing to go out and work.

Bill blames himself for:

_____(g)   getting Laura pregnant.

_____(h)   failing to send Laura any money from Las Vegas.

_____(i)   quitting school before he got a diploma.

_____(j)   not having any goals.

_____(k)   the breakup of their marriage.

Answers start on page 69.

LOOKING FOR SUPPORTING DETAILS

We have seen that a main idea by itself isn't very interesting. It leaves too many questions unanswered.

Here's another main idea by itself.

> Our trip was a real mess.

This main idea needs help. It needs more details to fill it out. The details should help answer questions we would probably ask as readers.

For example, the writer could answer these six questions about the messy trip:

Who? What? When? Where? Why? How?

The "what" question we already know a little about—a messy trip. The writer could go on this way.

> Our trip <u>last Saturday</u> was a real mess.

The "when" question has now been answered..
Much more can be added to the main idea.

> Our trip last Saturday night <u>to Fun Town</u> was a real disaster.

We can now answer the "where" question. Notice that the writer used the word "disaster." This says more than just "mess."

The writer can answer the "how" question by saying:

> Our trip last Saturday night to Fun Town in Ed Haynes' old Chevy was a real disaster.

All that is left now is the "why." Why was the trip such a disaster?

To answer this question the writer must come up with more than one sentence. Several details have to be added to support the main idea. Let's see how this might be done.

> Our trip last Saturday to Fun Town in Ed Haynes' old Chevy was a real disaster.
>
> We got only two miles out of town. Bang! An explosion we thought. Wrong. Just the Chevy's worn out rear tire blowing out.
>
> We took out the spare. There was no air in it. So Ed and his girl friend had to hitch to the nearest gas station for air. That took over two hours.
>
> When we got to Fun Town, the girls naturally were very hungry. We had to buy hot dogs and ice cream.
>
> This turned out to be a waste of money for my date, Linda. We rode the Loop-O-Plane first after eating. She threw up all over my pants and the Loop-O-Plane car. I had the workman hose me off before he cleaned the car out. Linda didn't want to do much the rest of the night.
>
> Ed and his date ate some cotton candy in front of Linda. She got sick again. I had

to sit with her on a bench the rest of the night. What a drag!

About ten in the evening it rained. Linda was sick again. We decided we might as well go home.

Right outside the park gate Ed was showing off. He plowed the Chevy through a big water puddle. Of course, the motor died on us.

Ed and I had to push the car to the side of the road. We were soaked to the skin. All we could do was sit and wait for the engine to dry. That took over an hour. So we didn't get home until nearly midnight.

What a disaster! Never again, I'll tell you.

The writer uses four different events to support the "why" of the main idea. Write them briefly in the blanks below. Tell why the trip was a real mess.

Event 1: _____

_____

Event 2: _____

_____

Event 3: _____

_____

Event 4: _____

_____

The events are

1. They had a flat tire and then had no air in the spare tire.
2. Linda got sick twice.
3. It started to rain.
4. The motor got wet and died out.

You do not have to have used these exact words. But you should be able to see how details are used to fill out a main idea.

Exercise 6

Read the following passage.

Harry M. was an Indian and an expert trapper. One night in 1928, he was camped four miles from the river where he had hidden his canoe.

The November air was chilly, so he wrapped up in a blanket. He fell asleep watching the fire.

Suddenly something scooped him up and threw him over its shoulder. It was a hairy creature. It smelled bad. It seemed to be seven feet tall and very strong. Harry was too scared to move.

The creature carried Harry three miles and set him down against a cold rock. He had lost his blanket. Harry shivered in his long underwear.

At daylight Harry found himself in a small cave. Twenty hairy creatures surrounded him. They looked like apes with black hair.

They didn't harm Harry. They liked to touch him and tug at his underwear.

Harry noticed a pile of bones nearby, and he almost panicked. He thought of only one thing—escape.

In the afternoon many of the creatures left, perhaps to search for food. The others lost interest in Harry. Here was his chance.

Harry dashed toward the river to his canoe. Passing his campsite, he paddled the canoe into the cold night.

At 3 A.M. Father Tonio at the village mission heard wild screams. Hurrying to the water, Father Tonio and the villagers found Harry in the canoe. He was nearly frozen, exhausted and wore only his torn underwear. They carried him to the hospital.

Father Tonio nursed Harry for three weeks. During this time Harry's hair turned white. He never went back to trapping. He left all his valuable tools at the camp.

How can we explain what happened to Harry? A lie? A nightmare? Was he crazy? Drunk? Or are there really creatures like these in the forests.

Remember the story's details as you do this exercise. Put a check mark (✔) in front of the correct ending for each statement.

1. Harry M. was an
   _____(1)   expert Indian hunter.
   _____(2)   expert Indian paddler.
   _____(3)   expert Indian scout.
   _____(4)   expert Indian trapper.
   _____(5)   expert Indian guide.

2. Harry set up a camp about
   _____(1)   20 miles from his village.
   _____(2)   12 miles from the river.
   _____(3)   four miles from the river.
   _____(4)   four miles from his village.
   _____(5)   12 miles from his village.

3. Harry M. slept in his
   _____(1)   underwear and a sleeping bag.
   _____(2)   clothes and a blanket.
   _____(3)   clothes and a sleeping bag.
   _____(4)   underwear covered by a blanket.
   _____(5)   naked covered by a blanket.

4. The time of the year was
   _____(1)   late fall.
   _____(2)   late spring.
   _____(3)   late winter.
   _____(4)   early spring.
   _____(5)   early winter.

5. The creature carried Harry on its shoulder for about
   _____(1)   five miles.
   _____(2)   three miles.
   _____(3)   three hours.
   _____(4)   two hours
   _____(5)   five hours.

6. The 20 creatures acted
   _____(1)   afraid of Harry.
   _____(2)   kindly toward Harry.
   _____(3)   mean toward Harry.
   _____(4)   curious about Harry.
   _____(5)   nasty toward Harry.

7. Harry almost panicked because of
    _____(1)   the cold weather.
    _____(2)   a pile of old bones.
    _____(3)   his hunger.
    _____(4)   the creatures pulling his underwear.
    _____(5)   being alone.

8. Harry was able to escape when
    _____(1)   no creature was left at their camp.
    _____(2)   the creatures went to sleep.
    _____(3)   many creatures left to hunt for food.
    _____(4)   only the smallest creatures were left in camp.
    _____(5)   Father Tonio came to rescue him.

9. Because of the kidnapping, Harry M.
    _____(1)   gave up trapping in that part of the country.
    _____(2)   gave up trapping completely.
    _____(3)   never got his normal health back.
    _____(4)   took a job as a hunting guide close to the village.
    _____(5)   went camping again to get over his fear.

10. The writer of the story feels that Harry's story is
    _____(1)   mostly lies.
    _____(2)   a crazy one.
    _____(3)   a nightmare.
    _____(4)   made up.
    _____(5)   none of these.

Answers start on page 70.

Exercise 7

Read this passage.

Today basketball fans can watch seven-foot men "stuff" the ball through the hoop easily. All they have to do is stretch up and drop it through. These big men are heroes to thousands of people.

But 80 years ago many athletes would not be caught playing basketball. The reason? They did not think the new game was manly enough. They did not think it was a real sport. No body contact was allowed.

William Naismith, the father of basketball, was a gym teacher at Springfield College in Massachusetts. His classes played football and soccer in the fall. They played baseball in the spring. Naismith needed an indoor game for the winter.

Naismith hung a peach basket of thin wood at each end of the gym. He divided his class into two teams and used a soccer ball. He made up 43 rules for his new game.

At first, whenever a team shot a basket, the game had to stop. Someone had to climb a ladder and take the ball out of the basket. But cutting out the bottom of the basket solved this problem.

Soon the number of players was cut down to five. A board with an iron hoop on it took the place of each basket. The new basket stuck out from the wall. This kept players from crashing into the wall.

More and more players began to like the game. Basketball has spread around the world. Other nations have seven-footers. The Russians even have a seven-foot woman player.

The big teams of today have steel hoops and fancy glass backboards to shoot at. Imagine a seven-footer trying to stuff the ball into a peach basket nailed to the wall.

Read the two lists of words below. Match the two lists by drawing a line from the words of list A to the words of list B that finish each sentence correctly.

A	**B**

1. Dr. William Naismith   (a) a seven-foot woman player.

2. Peach baskets   (b) was the first ball used in basketball games.

3. Russia has   (c) wrote 43 rules for the game of basketball.

4. To take the ball out of the baskets   (d) kept players from crashing into the walls.

5. A soccer ball   (e) cuts the number of players down to five.

6. Iron hoops   (f) ladders at each end of the gym were used.

7. Many athletes first thought that basketball   (g) took the place of the peach baskets.

8. Backboards with hoops that stuck out   (h) was the reason basketball was started.

9. The need for a winter sport   (i) was not a real sport.

10. A rule of modern basketball   (j) were used to shoot at when the game first started.

Answers start on page 70.

Exercise 8

Read this story.

Human beings have managed to wipe out many birds and animals during their history. Gone are the dodo bird and the passenger pigeon.

Others are now called "endangered" because they have

almost disappeared. These include the falcon, the condor, the grizzly bear and many others.

But one animal is not endangered by human beings— the tough coyote. The coyote has been able to get used to humans. They can even live near big cities.

People have tried to shoot them and poison them. People have trapped them and tried to starve them. But the tough coyote still lives on.

The coyote looks something like a German police dog. They weigh from 18 to 30 pounds. A coyote lives from 10 to 18 years. They can eat almost anything—mice, rats squirrels, rabbits, rattlesnakes and skunks. Even insects, berries and rotten meat can be food for the coyote.

The coyote lives in old rabbit or badger holes. They just dig the holes bigger and move their families in. If one home fills with fleas or becomes dangerous, the family moves again.

Each spring the female gives birth to a litter of eight to ten pups. She nurses and feeds them for the first month only. Then they have to join their parents in hunting for food. By fall the pups are on their own.

During times of food shortages, coyotes have a natural way of keeping down the number of mouths to feed. They don't have any young.

The coyote is smart and hard to catch. They can live near cities like Los Angeles or New York and get along well. Even cars on highways don't hit coyotes often. While some birds and animals have become endangered species, the coyote seems too tough to die out.

Write two facts about each of the following from this passage.

1. Two birds or animals that human beings have wiped out:
    (a) _____
    (b) _____

2. Two birds or animals that are now endangered:

   (a) _____

   (b) _____

3. Two ways human beings have tried to kill coyotes:

   (a) _____

   (b) _____

4. Two things that coyotes can eat:

   (a) _____

   (b) _____

5. Two facts about how the coyote looks:

   (a) _____

   (b) _____

6. Two facts about the coyote's home:

   (a) _____

   (b) _____

7. Two facts about the female's way of raising the young:

   (a) _____

   (b) _____

Answers start on page 71.

REMEMBERING DETAILS

We have talked about how writers use details to support their main ideas, but knowing how details are used won't do you any good unless you can remember the details. Questions about what you read often ask you to recall details from a passage. We will now talk about some ways you can remember the details you read.

Make Mind Pictures and Mind Sounds

When your friend does or says something funny, it is often easy for you to remember it. When it happens, you notice how your friend's face looks. You hear his or her words and the tone of voice. You see how your friend moves. If you tell someone else about it later, all those things you saw and heard may run through your mind. Let's call them mind pictures and mind sounds. Mind pictures and mind sounds help you to remember things.

When you read something, you should make mind pictures and mind sounds. Don't just read the words. Make a picture in your mind. Try to see what the words are saying. Hear what is said.

Usually a writer gives you clues to help you see and hear.

———————————

Read the following passage. See and hear while you read. Answer the questions about the passage.

It took me seven months to understand why Sharma never smiled. She smiled, but always a closed-lipped smile. Her thin face deserved a wide smile. Her eyes were the most outstanding feature in her face. They were deep brown and almond-shaped, sometimes sad. Her high cheekbones set her eyes apart from her mouth and chin.

When I first met Sharma, she was looking for a job. The day she got a job was the day I found out why she never really smiled.

I congratulated her in a funny way. She started to throw back her head and laugh. But she stopped herself.

Rather, she laughed the way someone laughs when caught with a full mouth. She fought to keep her lips closed. She was happy that with her job came a free dental plan. Sharma was missing teeth.

Without looking back at the passage, answer these questions. Write your answers in the blanks provided.

1. What color were Sharma's eyes? _____
2. What was Sharma's smile like? _____
3. Was Sharma's face thin or round? _____
4. What sound could you "hear" at the end of the story?

_____

Check your answers:

1. Sharma's eyes were brown.
2. Sharma's smile was closed-lipped.
3. Sharma's face was thin.
4. Sharma's laugh.

If you made a mind picture of Sharma as your read, you probably could answer each of those questions easily.

Put Yourself in the Situation

It is hard to read about ideas, events, places or people that are completely unknown to you. It is much easier to read your hometown newspaper. If you read about something that happened to someone you know, or in a place you know, it is easy to make pictures. If you are reading about a strange person, however, it's not so easy to make pictures. You need to use your imagination.

Try putting yourself in the situation. To do that, you need to pay close attention to every detail.

Read the following sentences. Put yourself in the situation. Look for the answer to this question while you are reading: Why did they lose the battle? Find three reasons.
The sentences:

> The heat overcame them. They had no strength to fight on and began to retreat. They gave up a lot of desert territory.

If you put yourself in the situation, you can see or feel yourself wearing a military uniform. You can see yourself on a desert, hot and tired. And then you can imagine yourself and your comrades turning back. With all those pictures, it is easy to see why the battle was lost.
"You" were
1. hot and
2. tired, so you
3. turned back.

Those are the three reasons.
Even though you may never have been in a military uniform fighting on a desert, you can imagine it.
To understand a person's emotions when you read, imagine that something like the situation you are reading about happened to you.

Now read the following and try to imagine the emotions of the person:

> Unemployment checks had stopped four weeks ago for Eligio. He was getting desperate. He'd been looking for a job for six months. Nothing. Then he saw an ad for people with his skills—exactly his skills! His heart began to beat a little faster. He called. Yes, they would like to interview him.
> He went to the place, took tests and was interviewed. The man said he had passed all the tests and that he liked his background. He would let him know in a week.

Eligio was sure he had the job. On Friday the man called. "Will you accept the job at $200 a week?"

"Will I! Yes! Thank you. Thank you!" He couldn't stop thinking about it all weekend. On Monday he went in to sign papers so he could start work.

On one paper was the question, "Have you ever been convicted of a felony or a misdemeanor, except for traffic violations?" He had once been a foolish youth and stolen a car for a joyride, but that was many years before. He answered "yes." He knew he could explain if he had to.

He turned the papers in. A few minutes later the interviewer came to him looking upset. The policy of the company was never to hire a convicted person for that particular job. The job was labeled "sensitive." The man was sorry, but there was nothing he could do.

Eligio was so let down he wasn't sure what he would do. One childish mistake years ago cost him his only chance in six months.

Here is a shortened list of the events in the story. Next to each event is a blank. Pick a word from the list of Emotions and Feelings that matches how Eligio must have felt at each point. Write that word in the blank. Use each word only once. There are more Emotions and Feelings words than you will need.

Emotions and Feelings

1. Eligio had not found a job. _____

desperate
encouraged
angry

2. He saw the ad. _____

overjoyed
let down

3. He left the interview. _____

loving
bitter
depressed

4. The man called on Friday. _____

hopeful

5. The man spoke to him after he filled out the papers. _____

6. He left. _____

Check yourself:

1. Desperate. He was getting desperate, as the story says, because he had been unemployed so long.

2. Encouraged or hopeful. Seeing the ad made him feel encouraged. Maybe he had a chance.

3. Hopeful or encouraged. Since he passed all the tests and the interviewer liked his background, he felt hopeful that he would get the job. (The story says he was "sure," but, of course, he could not be "sure" until the call came. We must understand "sure" to mean "very hopeful.")

4. Overjoyed. He got the job and felt overjoyed.

5. Let down. When he heard he could not be given the job he was very let down.

6. Depressed. As a few minutes passed and the news sank in, he felt worse and worse. He wasn't sure what he would do.

Nothing in the story suggests that Eligio got angry at anyone. (He may have become angry with himself, the interviewer or the company later, but the story doesn't go that far.)

Nowhere does the story suggest that Eligio felt loving. (That doesn't mean that he was not, but it isn't said.)

Eligio may have grown to feel bitter as more time passed and more bad luck came his way. The story doesn't show that, however.

Relate to Something You Already Know

Making mind pictures and mind sounds is a way to remember. Putting yourself in the situation is another good way. You've just practiced both ways. They are good for some reading. They work best on things you like or know about. They work very well on things about other real people. They work well on things you're starting to become interested in.

But, let's face it. Not everything you read is highly interesting. Right? Sometimes you have to read things—like this sentence, maybe—just because you have to. So, how can you best remember "not-so-interesting" details?

The best thing to do is this: if possible, relate what you must remember to something you already know. For example: If you read that an important event happened in 1965, think how old you were then. That will help you to remember the date.

If you read about the life of a king of Egypt, think about pictures of Egypt you have seen. Or, think of TV shows you've seen about Egypt. That will help you to create a mind picture.

To sum up: The most important thing to do when you read is smell . . . touch . . . hear . . . see . . . taste . . . become afraid . . . get angry . . . laugh . . . cry . . . worry . . . say, "Wow!" . . . pretend you're there. Get involved with what you're reading and you will remember much more of it.

PRACTICE REMEMBERING DETAILS

Four reading passages follow. Try to remember as much as you can about what you read. Answer the questions about each passage.

- Try not to look back when you are answering questions.

- Make mind pictures and mind sounds.
- Put yourself in the situation.
- Relate the passage to something you already know.

Do one at a time.

Exercise 9

Read the story below.

A strange wind starts to blow from the Pacific Ocean each winter and spring. It's called a chinook. It blows across the U.S. from west to east. Coming off the ocean, it is warm and wet air. It moves fast. It climbs up the mountains in Washington and Oregon. When the chinook reaches a certain height, it drops all its moisture as rain or snow. It keeps blowing east across the mountains. It stays warm. Then it comes roaring down to the plains like a hot locomotive. Because the wind is hot, and now dry, it absorbs any moisture in its way. It comes down across the plains of Wyoming and Colorado. There may already be a foot of snow on the ground. The temperature may be 20°F. When the chinook comes, sometimes at 100 miles per hour, the temperature will shoot up to 60°F. or 70°F. All the snow melts in an hour or so. The wind keeps going east. It is warm and moist again.

1. Where does a chinook start blowing? _____

   _____

2. A chinook climbs the mountains in Washington and Oregon. What is the wind like then? Check two:
   ___ cool   ___ 20°F.   ___ dry   ___ 70°F.
   ___ wet   ___ warm

3. How does the wind sound when it comes down the eastern side of the mountains? _____

    _____

4. How fast might a chinook blow? Check one:
    ___ 20 mph   ___ 60 mph   ___ 70 mph
    ___ 100 mph

5. The wind comes into Colorado and Wyoming. If there is snow on the ground, what two things will happen:

    (a) _____

    (b) _____

    Answers start on page 72.

Exercise 10

Read the following passage.

I heard about a man who worked in a roundhouse. Trains came in there for repairs. Or they sat there till their next trip. Sometimes they switched onto different tracks.

In the middle of the roundhouse was a turntable. Locomotives came in on one track and rode onto the turntable. The table turned and the locomotive ran off on a different track.

The man was working on the coupler on the front of a freight car. A locomotive was on the turntable. It was being turned so that it could back up to pick up the freight car. The man was working so hard that he didn't hear the locomotive backing up. The cars coupled right through his hips.

He laughed and yelled to the driver, "Come on, Sam! I can't work this way. Pull that engine out of here!" He must not have felt any pain at all. He was in shock. When the cars were uncoupled, his body fell in two pieces on the track.

1. What are three reasons trains come into roundhouses?

    (a) _____

    (b) _____

    (c) _____

2. What is the purpose of a turntable in a roundhouse?

    _____

    _____

Put a check mark in front of the correct answer.

3. Where was the man when he was killed?
    _____(1)   standing on the turntable
    _____(2)   standing by the freight car
    _____(3)   standing with Sam in the locomotive
    _____(4)   lying on the turntable tracks
    _____(5)   sitting in the freight car

4. Why did the man die?
    _____(1)   He was run over by the locomotive
    _____(2)   He died of fright
    _____(3)   He fell under the freight car
    _____(4)   He was cut in two
    _____(5)   He had a heart attack

Answers start on page 72.

Exercise 11

Read the following passage.

In a certain developing country there are very few classrooms or teachers. That country has to be very strict about who goes on in school. There is only one senior class in the whole country. That class can take no more than 40 students. Therefore, in any year, only 40 students can graduate. There is a way to choose the 40 who will complete their 13th year.

It starts after the 3rd grade. All students in the country take the same test when they finish the 3rd grade. Only the top third go on to the 4th grade. The same thing happens after the 6th, 9th, 11th, and 12th grades. So, if about 10,000 students enter first grade, only about 40 will finish the 13th year. They are the only ones who graduate.

Answer these questions about what you read.

1. How many high school senior classes are there in this country?

    _____

2. How many students are in each senior class?

    _____

3. After certain grades, a test is given. What fraction of the students go from one grade to the next after each test?

    _____

4. How many students would have to begin 1st grade so that about 40 will finish high school?

    _____

5. How many years does it take to graduate in this country?

    _____

6. If someone graduates, how many times has he passed the test to go to the next grade? (You may look back at the passage for help with this answer.)

Answers start on page 73.

Exercise 12

Read the passage.

The meanings of many words have very interesting stories. One such word is the word "sincere." It is made up of two Latin words: "sine" and "cere." "Sine" means "without"; "cere" means "wax." Therefore, "sine cere" means "without wax." Today "sincere" means "honest" or "true." This story is about how "without wax" and "true" are similar.

Picture the columns around the temples and palaces of ancient Rome. They were mostly made of marble. But, even then, some builders cheated on construction. They hollowed out a very big column. Then they used the part taken out to make a smaller column. The big, hollow column was put in place. The center was filled with wax.

As time passed, the marble of any column cracked in the heat. If no wax ran through the crack, it was a "true" marble column. It was "without wax." It was "sine cere." If wax ran out of the crack, people would know it was not a true marble column. They had been cheated.

So, even today we think of "sincere" as being "true." We may even say, "She gave me a sincere compliment. It was not a hollow compliment."

Answer the following.
1. From which language does our word "sincere" come?

---

2. Columns on Roman temples were

     _____(1)   all the same size.

     _____(2)   different sizes.

     _____(3)   The passage says nothing about it.

     _____(4)   made of wax.

     _____(5)   made of wood.

3. The word "cere" means

     _____(1)   without.

     _____(2)   true.

     _____(3)   wax.

     _____(4)   column.

     _____(5)   honest.

4. Is this true or false? Only the columns with wax inside cracked.

     _____True

     _____False

Answers start on page 73.

REVIEW EXERCISES—UNDERSTANDING PARAGRAPHS

The Review Exercises will give more practice using everything you learned in this unit.

Read each passage and answer the questions that follow.

Review Exercise 1

The animals that are most disliked today are the snake and the bat. Just name them and you will make many people shiver.

Of these two, the bat is more feared than the snake. Some people make pets of snakes, but who ever heard of a pet bat?

The bat brings up mind pictures of darkness, ghosts, witches and even blood-sucking vampires.

The bat's looks are against him. The world's only flying mammal, he's a member of the rat family. The faces of some bats look like bears'. Others look like tiny bulldogs or horses. Their noses seem punched in like the nose of a boxer who has fought too many times.

The bodies of some types of bats are only two inches long. The biggest are a foot long.

The bat doesn't have wings like birds. His front legs are connected to his body by a thin layer of skin. The smaller bats have a wingspread of one foot. The bigger ones can spread their wings out to seven feet.

The old saying, "Blind as a bat," is true. The bat depends on his mouth and ears to fly in the dark. He opens his mouth and makes high-pitched sounds. These sounds bounce off objects around the bat and return to his ears. He can keep from bumping into objects this way.

The bat hunts insects all night and returns home at dawn. He sleeps upside down, hanging by his hind legs. He wraps his front legs around himself like a blanket.

The bat is a creature of the darkness. Like Dracula, he goes back to his "grave" in daylight. He comes to life when darkness comes.

1. Put a check mark in front of the main idea of this passage.

   _____(1)   The bat is a lot like Dracula in the movies.

   _____(2)   Many people keep snakes as pets.

   _____(3)   The bat, like the snake, is disliked and feared by most people because of how it looks and lives.

_____(4)   The bat is a creature of the darkness.

_____(5)   Snakes and bats can make most people shiver.

Write T for true in front of those sentences below that are true. Write F for false in front of those that are false.

_____ 2.   The bat's body can grow from one inch to seven feet in length.

_____ 3.   The bat is actually a member of the same family as the rat.

_____ 4.   The faces of some bats look like bears, while others look like bulldogs.

_____ 5.   A bat sees with his mouth and ears instead of his eyes.

_____ 6.   The bat is a daytime creature and a mammal.

_____ 7.   The bat sleeps hanging upside down.

_____ 8.   The bat's wings are similar to a bird's wings.

_____ 9.   The bat reminds people of ghosts, witches and vampires.

Answers start on page 73.

Review Exercise 2

The left-handed person runs into problems everywhere. He or she finds out quickly that we live in a right-handed world.

Take, for example, the simple act of shaking hands. A child learns from the beginning the right way to do it. If the child is left-handed, it seems correct to shake hands that way. Right away someone says, "You don't shake with your left hand. That's not proper. Use your right hand." The child's natural hand, the left, isn't acceptable.

At school the left-hander tries to learn to write. But the way we write is made for right-handers. The child may even have to try to write on one of those one-armed desks. Most likely all the arms are on the right side. It is rare that the classroom will have a left-handed desk.

If the left-hander goes to eat at a long table in the cafeteria, he or she must take care in finding a seat. Sitting in the middle of the long table may cause the left-hander to bump elbows with the person nearby. The left-hander must sit at the end of the table to keep from bumping other people's elbows.

When the left-hander goes to church there are more problems. There is a Bible story about sheep and goats. The sheep are good; the goats are bad. The story says that God is going to separate the good from the bad. And how will it be done? The good sheep will go to God's right hand. The bad goats will end up on His left hand. Imagine what the left-hander thinks of this. Being left-handed must be evil.

Wherever the left-hander turns, he or she is made to feel like a second-class citizen in a right-handed world.

1.   The main idea of this passage is:_____

_____

In the blanks below describe the problems that the left-hander has with each of the following activities.

2.   Shaking hands:_____

_____

3.   Writing at school:_____

_____

4. Sitting at desks in school:_____

_____

5. Eating at long tables:_____

_____

6. Applying the sheep and goats story at church:_____

_____

Answers start on page 74.

Review Exercise 3

Hattie McDaniel spent most of her movie career wearing a black blouse, a white apron and a white bandana on her head. She seemed always to play a maid or a "mammy" for a Southern family.

Many black people asked her in the 1930s and '40s, "Why do you always play maids? It's bad for our race to do that all the time."

Hattie spoke right up. "I'd rather play a maid for $7,000 a week than really be one for $7 a week."

Hattie McDaniel knew how to be a real maid. Many times she had worked as a maid to earn a living. The pay then was $1 a day plus room and board.

Hattie was born in Wichita, Kansas in 1893. She was the youngest child of two former slaves. Very early in her life, the family moved to Denver, Colorado.

Here two of her brothers and a sister sang and danced on street corners to earn a little money. Hattie joined them by doing just what her sister did.

Hattie was left alone when her brothers and sister moved from Denver. She took maid jobs during the daytime. At night she sang in nightclubs and in vaudeville shows. She wrote her own music and songs. She even got parts in musicals like "Showboat."

By now her brothers and sister had gone to Hollywood. They acted in the movies. So they sent for Hattie. She went to work again as a real maid and worked part-time in films.

Soon she was acting with all the famous stars of those times: Shirley Temple, Jean Harlowe, Mae West and Clark Gable. Naturally, she was able to give up being a real maid.

The climax of her career in movies was winning an Oscar for the maid she played in "Gone with the Wind." People were again upset that she took the part. Hattie answered, "What did you expect me to play? Clark Gable's leading lady?"

Read the following sentences. Put a check in front of the correct ending for the sentence.

1. Hattie McDaniel was the daughter of
    _____(1)   two former slaves.
    _____(2)   two former servants.
    _____(3)   two former movie stars.
    _____(4)   two former stage actors.
    _____(5)   two former farmers.

2. In most of the movies Hattie made, she wore
    _____(1)   a red bandana, white apron and a turban.
    _____(2)   a white blouse, white apron and a white bandana.
    _____(3)   a white bandana, a black blouse and a white apron.
    _____(4)   a black blouse, black bandana and a black apron.
    _____(5)   a white uniform, black apron and a turban.

3. Many black people didn't think Hattie should play a maid because

_____(1)   there was no money in it.

_____(2)   it hurt her acting career.

_____(3)   it was bad for all race groups.

_____(4)   it was bad for the black race.

_____(5)   she wasn't good for the role.

4. Hattie was born in 1893 in

_____(1)   Wichita, Kansas.

_____(2)   Denver, Colorado.

_____(3)   Atlanta, Georgia.

_____(4)   Kansas City, Kansas.

_____(5)   Chicago, Illinois.

5. Hattie moved to Hollywood because

_____(1)   she wanted to get away from home.

_____(2)   she could make more money there.

_____(3)   people had more maids there.

_____(4)   her brothers and sister sent for her.

_____(5)   she was asked to play a leading role.

6. As small children, the McDaniels earned money by

_____(1)   singing and dancing on street corners.

_____(2)   playing drums and horns on street corners.

_____(3)   ringing bells on street corners.

_____(4)   selling magazines and newspapers on street corners.

_____(5)   cooking and cleaning in people's homes.

7. One of Hattie's talents was

_____(1) tap dancing.

_____(2) writing music and songs.

_____(3) ballet dancing.

_____(4) making records of her songs.

_____(5) playing the piano.

8. A real maid in Hattie's time earned

_____(1) $2 a day and board.

_____(2) board, room and $5 a week.

_____(3) $25 a week.

_____(4) $1 a day, plus room and board.

_____(5) board, room and $7 a week.

9. Hattie earned an Oscar for her part in the movie

_____(1) "The Bad and the Beautiful."

_____(2) "Gone with the Wind."

_____(3) "Jaws."

_____(4) "True Grit."

_____(5) "Guess Who's Coming to Dinner."

10. The sentence that best tells the main idea of this passage is

_____(1) Hattie McDaniel made good money by working hard in the movies.

_____(2) Hattie McDaniel, playing many different roles, worked her way up to an Oscar in Hollywood.

_____(3) Hattie McDaniel worked hard and made the best of the opportunities that came her way.

_____(4) Hattie McDaniel proved it was easy to go from being a real maid to acting as a maid.

_____(5) Hattie McDaniel worked hard but never had a chance to show her real talents.

Answers start on page 74.

Review Exercise 4

John and I were talking in front of his apartment on 110th Street. We heard screams from across the street. We ran over to see what was going on.

On the top step of the apartment building we found Linda Garcia. She had cuts and bruises on her face. Blood was running from her nose. Her clothes were torn.

"What happened, Linda?" asked John.

In a shaky voice she said, "I was walking down the stairs. This guy jumped me. Tore my clothes. I scratched his face and screamed. He knocked me down and ran."

We helped Linda back to her apartment. Her older sister put her in bed. "I'll call the clinic. Someone will come and check her."

"Who did it, Linda?" I asked.

"I don't know. He was fat. Had a beard and a scar on his forehead."

"I know him," said John. "Don't worry, Linda." We left.

Outside, I asked, "You know him, John?"

"Sounds like this guy who hangs around all the time on 112th Street. Let's get him."

I wasn't sure. "Maybe we ought to call the cops."

"It'll take too long, and they won't do nothing. Are you afraid?"

"No. Let's go."

We spotted the man on 112th. We ran toward him, but he saw us coming. Too fat to run, he pulled a handgun.

"Stay away from me!" He took three wild shots.

I saw John drop. I knelt down beside him. The blood was staining his shirt around the shoulder.

At the hospital writing his report, the cop asked, "Why didn't you guys call us? Look at what happens when you take the law into your own hands."

Lying in the bed, John felt his bandages. "Maybe you're right."

1. The main idea of the passage is: _____
_____

2. Mark T for true and F for false next to the following facts from this story.

_____(a) John and the writer heard shots from across the street.

_____(b) The writer was afraid to go and see what had happened because he might get into trouble.

_____(c) Linda Garcia had been attacked by a man on the stairs of her apartment building.

_____(d) Linda had scared the man away by screaming and scratching him.

_____(e) Linda's attacker was fat and had a beard.

_____(f) John knew the attacker and wanted to go after him.

_____(g) The writer was also very eager to go get the attacker.

_____(h) John felt the police would help them find the attacker.

_____(i) The attacker fired his gun because he was too fat to run.

_____(j) John got hit in the right leg by a wild shot.

_____(k) The policeman at the hospital told the two friends that they shouldn't take the law into their own hands.

_____(l) John had to agree with the policeman.

Answers start on page 74.

Review Exercise 5

Suppose you see a friend of yours walking down the street. "How are you?" you ask.

He answers, "Everything's real george."

If you don't understand what he's saying, you are probably in your twenties or thirties.

"Real george" was a slang term used in the 1950s. It meant something like cool, neat or very fine.

Sometime you might be watching a late movie on TV. It could be a 1939 movie about gangsters. The head gangster could say to one of his mugs, "We need geetus to get the roscoes!" Of course you don't know what he's talking about.

The words mugs, geetus and roscoes don't seem to be English. You have to find a way to get their meanings. Mugs means small-time tough guys. Geetus means money and roscoes are guns.

This example shows you one of the big problems with slang. It changes so fast you can hardly keep up with it. Ten years from now the slang we use today will sound silly, and some people won't understand what it means.

If we use slang over and over again, it can become a real word in Standard English. Once the term "hot dog" was slang for frankfurter. But now it's a term that everybody uses and understands.

Many people try to use slang to show that they are "with it." But there's a danger in using it too much. At anytime, today's "with it" can become as meaningless or silly as yesterday's "real george."

Answer the questions below by filling in the blanks.

1.   The main idea is:_____

_____

2. If a reader doesn't understand the words "real george," the reader is probably_____.

3. To many readers the slang words <u>mugs</u>, <u>geetus</u> and <u>roscoe</u> are not like_____words.

4. The slang term "real george" means_____.

5. (a) A <u>mug</u> means_____.

    (b) <u>Geetus</u> is_____.

    (c) And a <u>roscoe</u> is a_____.

6. One big problem with slang is that it_____ fast.

7. Sometimes slang words are used so often they become _____words in the language.

ANSWERS AND EXPLANATIONS—UNDERSTANDING PARAGRAPHS

Exercise 1

Your answers may be a little different.

(1)   Topic: A new disco—Frisco's.
      Main Idea: The new disco, called Frisco's, is too expensive.
      Sentence number: (5)

(2)   Topic: Cable television
      Main Idea: Cable television has improved reception.
      Sentence number: (1)

(3)   Topic: Shepherds
      Main Idea: By instinct shepherds lick people's feet to help them relax.
      Sentence number: (7)

(4)   Topic: How "OK" began.
      Main Idea: Theodore Roosevelt may have started the use of "OK."
      Sentence number: (4)

Exercise 2

1.   (5) Buying used cars from friends is a gamble because there is no warranty on them.

2.   (a)   T
     (b)   T
     (c)   F; Debbie paid $850 for the used car.
     (d)   T
     (e)   F; the towing cost $25.

Exercise 3

1. You are taking a gamble if you buy a car <u>as is</u>. This means you accept the car with whatever may be wrong with it. The wording of your answer may be different but the idea should be the same.

2. 1. (e)   5. (c)
    2. (a)   6. (g)
    3. (f)   7. (d)
    4. (h)   8. (b)

Exercise 4

1. Laura's Main Idea: It can be a big mistake to get married when you're too young and have not finished your education. Your answer may be different, but the idea should be the same.

2. You should discuss your answers with a friend. There might be differences of opinion!
    (a) no   (f) yes or maybe
    (b) yes   (g) no
    (c) maybe   (h) yes
    (d) yes   (i) yes
    (e) yes   (j) yes

Exercise 5

1. Bill's Main Idea: A wife who is lazy and doesn't seem to work at anything might lose her husband.

2. You should discuss your answers with a friend. There might be differences of opinion!

(a)	yes	(f)	yes
(b)	yes	(g)	no
(c)	yes	(h)	yes
(d)	yes	(i)	no
(e)	no	(j)	no
		(k)	no

Exercise 6

1. (4) expert Indian trapper.
2. (3) four miles from the river.
3. (4) underwear covered by a blanket.
4. (1) late fall.
5. (2) three miles.
6. (4) curious about Harry.
7. (2) a pile of old bones.
8. (3) many creatures left to hunt for food.
9. (2) gave up trapping completely.
10. (5) none of these.

Exercise 7

1.	(c)	6.	(g)
2.	(j)	7.	(i)
3.	(a)	8.	(d)
4.	(f)	9.	(h)
5.	(b)	10.	(e)

Exercise 8

1. You may have written any two of these:
    (a) dodo bird
    (b) passenger pigeon
    (c) Bengal tiger

2. You may have any two of these:
    (a) falcon
    (b) condor
    (c) grizzly bear

3. You may have any two of these:
    (a) poisoned them
    (b) trapped them
    (c) shot them
    (d) starved them

4. You may have any two of these:
    (a) mice
    (b) rats
    (c) squirrels
    (d) rabbits
    (e) rattlesnakes
    (f) skunks
    (g) insects
    (h) berries
    (i) rotten meat

5. (a) It looks like a German police dog.
    (b) It weighs 18 to 30 pounds.

6. Any two of these would be correct:
    (a) It uses an old hole of a rabbit or badger.
    (b) It just digs it bigger.
    (c) It moves when its home becomes dangerous or fills
         with fleas.

7. Any two of these would be correct:
    (a) She feeds them for the first month only.
    (b) After the first month the pups join their parents in the hunt for food.
    (c) By fall the pups are on their own.
    (d) They will have no pups during food shortages.

Exercise 9

1. The Pacific Ocean
2. Warm, wet; All the other choices talk about the wind and weather on the eastern side of the mountains, not in Washington or Oregon.
3. It roars. Or it sounds like a roaring locomotive.
4. 100 mph. Only one speed is mentioned in the passage. The other numbers refer to temperatures.
5. Any two of these:
    (a) The snow will melt.
    (b) The temperature will rise.
    (c) The wind becomes moist again.

Exercise 10

1. (a) for repairs
    (b) to sit until their next trip
    (c) to be switched onto different tracks
2. Turntables switch locomotives onto different tracks by turning them.
3. (2) standing by the freight car
4. (4) He was cut in two.

Exercise 11

1. One
2. 40
3. One-third
4. 10,000
5. 13
6. Five. They take tests after these grades: 3rd, 6th, 9th, 11th, 12th.

Exercise 12

1. Latin
2. (2) The passage talks of both large and small columns.
3. (3) "Cere" means "wax" in Latin.
4. False. The passage says that any column could crack. Wax would run from those columns that had been hollowed out.

ANSWERS AND EXPLANATIONS—REVIEW EXERCISES

Review Exercise 1

1. (3)
2. F
3. T
4. T
5. T
6. F
7. T
8. F
9. T

Review Exercise 2

Your answers may be slightly different but the ideas should be the same.

1. The person who is left-handed runs into problems everywhere in this right-handed world.
2. The left-hander is taught it isn't proper to shake hands with the left hand.
3. The left-handed child is taught by a system made for right-handers.
4. Most often all of the desks are made for right-handers.
5. The left-handed person has to watch where he or she sits to keep from bumping the right-handers.
6. The goats were sent to sit at God's left hand. This makes the left-hander feel bad.

Review Exercise 3

1. (1)   6. (1)
2. (3)   7. (2)
3. (4)   8. (4)
4. (1)   9. (2)
5. (4)   10. (3)

Review Exercise 4

1. The main idea of the passage is that because the two friends tried to get the man who attacked Linda themselves, John was shot. They should have called the police. (You don't have to have these exact words.)

2. (a) F   (e) T   (i) T
    (b) F   (f) T   (j) F
    (c) T   (g) F   (k) T
    (d) T   (h) F   (l) T

Review Exercise 5

1. The main idea of the passage is that slang changes very
    fast. Yesterday's slang can often sound silly. (You need
    not have these exact words.)
2. a fairly young person
3. English
4. neat, cool or very fine
5. (a) small-time tough guy
    (b) money
    (c) gun
6. changes
7. real or standard

2 HOW DETAILS ARE ARRANGED

So far we have talked mostly about finding and stating the main idea of a paragraph or story. But a main idea cannot stand alone. It needs something more. The other sentences of a paragraph or the paragraphs of a story carry the details, facts and examples. These support and explain the main idea. Here you will see some of the different ways that writers arrange details. We will look at the order in which details come and at the relationships between details. We will see how details are ranked in importance. Knowing the ways that details are put into a paragraph will help you understand and remember what you read.

SEQUENCE—TIME, PLACE, IDEAS AND EVENTS

Sequence is the order in which things come. Monday is the day before Tuesday. Five comes after four. Sequence is also the order in which events happen in time. You must turn on a faucet before water will come out. Your baby sister was born two years after you were. The details, facts and examples the author uses to support the main idea are placed in a paragraph in a certain sequence. This order can be based on time, place, ideas or events.

Putting Things in Order by Time

One way a writer may write is in **chronological order.** All this means is that the writer has put something in order by time. It is the "real" order in which things happened in time. The event that happened first, goes first. The event that came next goes second, and so on. History books are good examples of writing in chronological order. They often start at a certain time and go on from there. Time is very important to the history book writer.

Time might also be very important in detective and mystery books and stories. The police or the TV detectives need to know the exact times different events happened. This can help solve crimes more quickly.

Knowing that a book or a story follows a time order can make it easier for us to read. We can notice dates coming one right after another. It is possible to draw a line for stories in time order, like this:

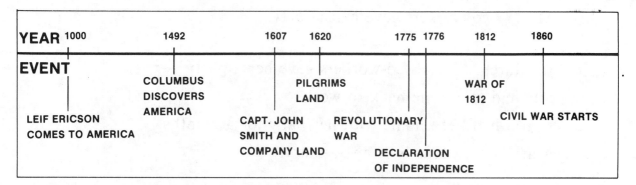

These lines are naturally called **time lines**.

A story can also be told in mixed-up time order. Writers don't always follow a straight time line. Mystery writers often start with the murder or the crime first. From there, they must try to let the reader know everything leading up to the murder.

The time lines for a murder story might look something like this:

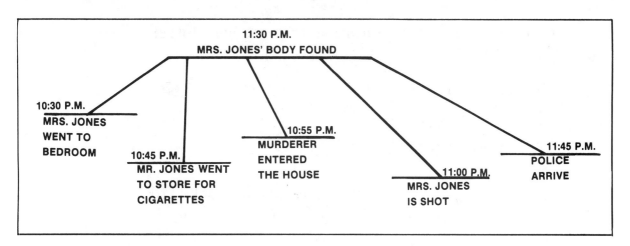

Whenever you read a story written in backward or mixed up order, try to see the events in your mind in a straight time order like a history book. You will understand the story and remember the details much more easily.

Here are two ways to tell the same story. Read each set of sentences. Number the sentences in each set from 1 to 4 to show which event came first, second and so on.

_____   Maria had a baby in January.
_____   She stayed home with the baby for 3 months.
_____   In March Maria went back to work.
_____   Maria's co-workers gave her a party.

_____   In March, Maria's co-workers gave her a party.
_____   She had just come back to work.
_____   Maria had been home with her baby for 3 months.
_____   Maria's baby was born in January.

The first telling of the story is in chronological order. You should have numbered the first group of blanks 1, 2, 3, 4. In the second telling of the story you should have numbered the blanks 4, 3, 2, 1. You see, the story was told backwards.

Read the following sentence. Then read its parts that are given below it. In the blanks next to the parts, write the numbers 1 to 3, to show the chronological order.

Mrs. Lerman said that Tim broke the vase her mother had made.

_____   Mrs. Lerman said
_____   that Tim broke the vase
_____   her mother had made.

You should have written the numbers in backward order—3, 2, 1. First, Mrs. Lerman's mother made the vase.

Second, Tim broke the vase. Third, Mrs. Lerman said that this happened.

Read the following story. Then go back and write the numbers 1 to 12 in the blanks to show the chronological order.

_____ Ted said

_____ that he tried to get in the house.

_____ His key wouldn't work

_____ because Ann had bolted the door from the inside.

_____ He rang the bell,

_____ but she didn't hear it.

_____ She had gone to sleep.

_____ So he went to a friend's house

_____ and called her on the telephone.

_____ That woke her.

_____ When he got back,

_____ she let him in.

This is the proper order for the numbers:

12, 3, 4, 1, 5, 6, 2, 7, 8, 9, 10, 11.

Chronologically, the events occurred in this order:

(1)   Ann bolted the door and
(2)   went to sleep.
(3)   Ted tried to get in, but
(4)   his key wouldn't open the door.
(5)   So he rang the bell, but
(6)   she didn't hear it.
(7)   He went to a friend's house and
(8)   called her on the telephone and
(9)   woke her.
(10) When he got back,
(11) she let him in.
(12) Later, he told the story.

Exercise 1

Read the following passage. Four sentences are underlined. In the spaces that follow the passage, copy the underlined sentences in chronological order. Put the first event on line 1 and so on.

Nearly 1,000 people in Nevada began to sue the government in the 1970s. Each of the 1,000 has been affected by medical problems. The problems include cancer, birth defects, sterility and miscarriages. The number of these problems among the 1,000 is very high. They blame the area where they live.

In the 1950s nearly 100 atomic bombs were dropped in Nevada. They were dropped between Las Vegas and the towns were these people lived. The bombs were always dropped when the wind blew away from Las Vegas. The wind blew straight toward the people who are suing. They believe the radiation from the bombs caused their illnesses.

1. _____

   _____

2. _____

   _____

3. _____

   _____

4. _____

   _____

Answers start on page 113.

Exercise 2

Read the following passage. Decide the chronological order of the sentences. Don't use the sentences in parentheses ( ). Write a number in each blank. The number 1 should be in the blank by what happened first; then 2, and so on.

_____ In the 1800s Anton Chekhov wrote a true story about a 9-year-old boy named Vanka.

_____ Vanka wrote a letter to his grandfather one Christmas. (His grandfather worked for some very rich country people in Russia. In the letter Vanka told about how he was being treated.)

_____ After his mother died, Vanka became the servant of a shoemaker in the city.

_____ As was common, he was beaten, starved and given too much work to do. (In the letter Vanka pleaded with his grandfather to get him out of there. He wanted to return to the country with his grandfather.)

_____ He had lived in the country before his mother died.

_____ When he finished the letter, he sealed it in an envelope.

_____ He had bought the envelope the day before and hidden it.

_____ On the outside he wrote his grandfather's name—nothing more.

_____ He dropped it in a mailbox in the middle of Moscow.

_____ He went to bed happy. (He was sure his grandfather would rescue him.)

Answers start on page 113.

Exercise 3

Read this story. There are 12 events which are underlined and marked with a letter. Write one letter under each of the numbers at the end of the story to show the chronological order.

Aunt Georgia—we love her, yes, we love her—but she can't get anything straight. She gets so excited about things that her tongue twists stories into pretzels. Sometimes I don't know where they start or end. When I met her at the bus station last week, she had a story. She was just returning from her niece's wedding. This is what she said. I hope you can straighten it out:

My dear, it was just the prettiest wedding I've ever seen. (a) The first thing I did was eat three shrimp cocktails before (b) your Uncle Bob Junior got there, you know. (c) I saw him put some shrimp in his suitcase, as usual. Anyway, after that, I ate...but, darling, I'm getting way ahead of myself! That was the reception! The wedding was first, of course. (She giggled.) (d) When Charlotte was coming down the aisle, everyone looked pleased. But then, of course, (e) I helped her put on her flowers. So, she was coming down the aisle and (f) her mother helped her get dressed. That was such a scene! (g) They couldn't find the veil. And then (h) when the cake was cut, the lights went out for a minute. (i) The groom was so nervous he couldn't find the ring and (j) the preacher had to slap him in the face to calm him down. And (k) when the lights came on, (l) someone had taken the first slice of cake....

You see how confused she gets! I don't have the strength to tell any more.

(1)	(2)	(3)	(4)	(5)	(6)	(7)	(8)	(9)	(10)	(11)	(12)
f	G	e	d	i	j	b	c	a	h	K	l

Answers start on page 114.

Putting Things in Order by Place

You have done a lot of work putting events in order by time. Often when you read, you will find that <u>places</u> are as important as <u>time</u>. Think again of history. Events happen at certain times. But they also happen in certain places.

Look at this time line from American history that we saw at the beginning of the unit.

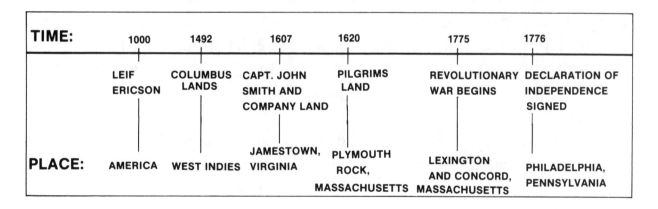

Place plays an important part in understanding what you read. It is tied together closely with time.

Exercise 4

The following story took place in one hour, in one place, on one night—Halloween. It is a true story that affected many people in different places. Notice as you read what happened in those places.

Today we have landed Viking spaceships on Mars. They have taken soil samples and color pictures. So far no one has seen any creatures on Mars, big or small, green or purple.

But 30 years ago on Halloween, thousands of people in the United States thought Martians had invaded the earth. That October night people were listening to a radio play from New York City. The play was called "War of the Worlds." It was put on by a young actor named Orson Welles.

In the play some Martians landed in Grover's Mill, New Jersey. They began killing humans with death rays and poison gas. Many listeners didn't know the broadcast was only a play.

The Martians headed for New York City. As they went, they sprayed a cloud of black gas. In real life, people fled their homes. They jammed the highways trying to escape. Police radios announced that the broadcast wasn't real. But that didn't do much good.

In Pittsburgh, Pennsylvania, a man came home and found his wife with a bottle of poison. She screamed and waved the poison. "I'd rather die this way than be killed by Martians!"

In Indianapolis, Indiana, a woman ran into a church service. She shouted, "New York has been destroyed. I just heard it on the radio! You all might as well go home to die! It's the end of the world."

Other people prayed and cried. They thought the end was here.

Orson Welles and those who put on the program were amazed at what had happened. They felt they had made it clear that the broadcast was just a play.

Many radio stations now replay the "War of the Worlds." The small town of Grover's Mill, New Jersey, still talks about the night the Martians landed.

Match the event with the place where it happened. Write the name of the place in the blank.

New York City
Pittsburgh, Pennsylvania
Grover's Mill, New Jersey
Indianapolis, Indiana
the planet Mars

1. (a) A church service in _____ was ended by a woman.
   (b) The invaders first landed in _____.
   (c) Viking spaceships have landed on _____ _____.
   (d) A woman in _____ threatened to take poison.
   (e) The play was broadcast from _____.

2. Complete the following sentences briefly.

   (a) Orson Welles was _____.

   _____.

   (b) Welles was very surprised because _____

   _____.

   (c) Many thousands thought the play was _____

   _____.

   (d) The play was broadcast on the _____

   _____.

(e)   It did no good, but the police tried to _____

_____.

Answers start on page 114.

Putting Things in Order by Ideas

Once in a while a person will get an idea at just the right time. The one idea will start a whole string of ideas. One seems to lead easily to another.

Other people hear of the ideas, like them and start to use them. Soon whole groups are following the ideas of one person.

In the following story, you will read how a man, who hardly knew one end of a horse from the other, became the movies' first cowboy star. From a very poor start the man came up with some of the ideas that other cowboy actors used after him.

Exercise 5

Read the story. Then complete the exercises that follow.

More than 70 years ago, Max Anderson walked into a stable to rent a horse. He had gotten a job playing a bandit in the first cowboy movie, "The Great Train Robbery." He started to climb on a horse.

"Hey, you!" shouted the stable man. "Don't get on the horse from that side."

"Why not?" asked Max.

"You try it. You'll find out."

Max climbed on the horse from the wrong side and rode off to where the cameras were shooting. During the first scene, the rented horse bucked Max. He had to become a bandit on foot.

This wasn't a very good start for the actor who would become our first cowboy. But Max didn't quit. He began starring in short, silent Westerns.

Max became the model for many cowboys in films. Later cowboys like Gene Autry, Roy Rogers, Clint Eastwood, Lorne Greene and John Wayne used Max's ideas. It was Max Anderson who did, for the first time, some of the things that would become standard for later cowboys. Max was the first to give himself a nickname—Bronco Billy. He always acted shy around the ladies. He'd just as soon kiss a horse as a woman. Of course, he could never marry and settle down. Bronco Billy never attacked anyone unless it was in self-defense. Of course, he had to be able to shoot a dime from a man's fingers at 50 yards. Naturally, the cowboy had to be able to ride a horse well. He rode forward and backward in the saddle. He had to ride hanging down by the horse's side. He had to jump off buildings and trees right into his saddle.

None of these things came easily to Bronco Billy. But he did become the cowboy that later actors copied. It was his ideas that were later to be used by all cowboys.

1. The following are events that led Bronco Billy to come up with some of his ideas on cowboy movies. Fill in the blanks with the correct words.

Max Anderson had to _____ his first horse from a stable. A worker there had to tell Max not to

_____

_____.

In the first scene of a movie called _____

_____ the horse

_____ Max off. So Max had to become a

_____ on foot. This was a poor start, but Max still became the movies' first _____.

2. Max Anderson started many ideas still used in cowboy movies. Briefly write in the blank the idea Max started about each word given.

Names: *Cowboy actors should have nicknames.*

(a) Women:_____

_____

(b) Fighting:_____

_____

(c) Horses:_____

_____

(d) Guns:_____

_____

Answers start on page 115.

Putting Things in Order by Events

Each person born into the world lives for a certain <u>time</u>. We live in certain <u>places</u>. And, of course, many things happen in a lifetime. These things we call <u>events</u>.

Often the events in a person's life make the person what he or she is. A person might suffer an accident and lose an arm or a leg. Such a tragic event can change that person's whole life.

Some big events can change the lives of thousands or even millions of people. Think, for instance, of a flood or a tornado that can destroy towns and cities. Think of a war that can affect millions the world over. Even what the president of a country does or doesn't do can change lives.

So you can say that events are very important in everyone's life. Sometimes the events make us. Other times we make the events.

Very often in reading, the events the author writes about and the order in which they happen are very important. You are about to read a story about the life of a famous baseball star, LeRoy "Satchel" Paige. Notice the order in which you read about the events of his life. The writer doesn't start at the beginning and go right to the end. He starts in 1948 and then skips back to 1906.

Also notice how Satchel caused some events in his life by doing certain things. Other events he didn't cause, but they changed his life.

Exercise 6

Read this story. Think about the order of the events.

More than 78,000 people were in Cleveland Stadium the night of August 20, 1948. They were eagerly waiting to see LeRoy "Satchel" Paige pitch for the Indians against the Chicago White Sox.

What was so unusual about Satchel Paige? Two things. He was 42 years old. He was the first black man ever to pitch in major league baseball.

Satchel was beginning a career at an age when most other players had already retired. Why was he coming to baseball in the majors so late? It was because he was black.

Until after World War II, no black players were allowed. They had to play in their own Negro leagues around the country. Many great baseball players missed the majors because they were black.

LeRoy Paige was the seventh child of a poor family. He was born in 1906 in Mobile, Alabama. He never had much schooling and went to work early, carrying suitcases, bags and satchels at the train station. That's where he got his nickname.

He learned to pitch by throwing rocks. He was too poor to own a baseball. He started hanging around the local baseball fields and getting into games.

One day he took some cheap toys from a store. For this crime he spent several years in a reform school. He played more there.

He got into professional baseball after he was released. For years he pitched in Negro leagues. Many times big league stars told him, "If you were only white!"

That night in 1948 in Cleveland, many laughed at the idea of a 42-year-old rookie. But Satchel shut out the White Sox, 1 to 0, with three hits.

He pitched in the majors into his fifties. Satchel believed in always looking forward. He often said, "Never look back. Something might be gaining on you!"

Read the ten events below from the passage. They are mixed up. Figure out the order in which the events happened. Start with the earliest and go to the latest. Write the letter of the first event by number 1; the second by 2; the third event by 3 and so on.

1. ____   (a) Satchel shuts out the Chicago White Sox in his first game in Cleveland, Ohio.

2. ____   (b) Satchel goes to reform school for taking some toys.

3. ____   (c) Satchel throws rocks because he is too poor to own a real baseball.

4. ____   (d) He is born in Mobile, Alabama in 1906.

5. ____   (e) Satchel gets his nickname from carrying suitcases at a train station.

6. ___   (f) Satchel was still pitching in the majors in his fifties.

7. ___   (g) He begins hanging around local ball fields and getting into games.

8. ___   (h) He becomes a pro player and pitches in Negro leagues.

9. ___   (i) The major leagues drop color rules against blacks after World War II.

10. ___   (j) Satchel often hears big league stars tell him, "If you were only white!"

Answers start on page 116.

RELATIONSHIPS

We began by saying that details, facts and examples can be arranged in a paragraph in many ways. We have shown that a writer may use sequences of time, place, ideas or events to arrange the details of the main topic. Now we will look at three kinds of relationships that writers may also use to arrange supporting details.

Seeing Cause and Effect Relationships

In a **cause and effect relationship,** one thing makes another thing happen. Or, one event or condition <u>causes</u> another one. The second event is the <u>effect</u> of the first.

In your reading, when you come to the word "because," keep your eyes open. It is a sign that a cause and effect relationship is being explained.

> Jorge couldn't call his girlfriend <u>because</u> he was stranded with a flat tire.

CAUSE: Jorge had a flat tire.

EFFECT: He couldn't call his girlfriend.

Because you did not do your household chores, I am angry.

CAUSE: You did not do your chores.

EFFECT: I'm angry.

The word "because" is not always needed to show a cause and effect relationship.

Maria's low opinion of herself has driven her to drink.

The cause and effect relationship is not as clearly stated here. The same idea can be said with the word "because."

Because Maria has a low opinion of herself, she has started drinking.

or

Maria has started drinking because she has a low opinion of herself.

CAUSE: Maria has a low opinion of herself.

EFFECT: She drinks.

You can see that there is more than one way to rewrite the sentence using "because."

Exercise 7

Re-write the following sentences using the word "because." There is more than one way to re-write the sentences correctly. Then, fill in the blanks by the words *Cause* and *Effect*.

1.. Congress cut spending for job programs. Many people still have no work.

_____

_____

Cause:_____

Effect:_____

2. Some religions say that men can have many wives, so they marry two or more.

_____

_____

Cause: _____

Effect: _____

3. They studied and did well on the test.

_____

_____

Cause: _____

Effect: _____

4. The balloon burst after Ned stuck it with a pin.

_____

_____

Cause: _____

Effect: _____

5. Agnes lost 15 pounds when she stopped eating meat.

_____

_____

Cause: _____

Effect: _____

Answers start on page 116.

Exercise 8

Now read this story. Find at least three cause and effect relationships in it. Write them in the spaces.

It happened in the days before mail service and telephones. A rich farmer took a long trip. When he came home, he asked the first field hand he saw what had happened while he was away. This is how their talk went:

Field hand: Well, the dog died.

Farmer: The dog died! How?

Field hand: The horses ran over him when they got scared and ran out of the barn.

Farmer: What scared the horses? Why did they run?

Field hand: They were running from the flames when the barn caught fire.

Farmer: My God! How did the barn catch fire?

Field hand: Well, sir, flames jumped over from the house and caught the barn on fire.

Farmer: From the House! Did the house burn down, too?

Field hand: Yep. The house is gone, too.

Farmer: How on Earth did the house burn down?

Field hand: You see, one of the candles around your wife's casket fell over and caught the house on fire.

1.   Cause:_____

    Effect:_____

2.   Cause:_____

    Effect:_____

3.   Cause:_____

    Effect:_____

Answers start on page 117.

Seeing Relationships of Comparison and Contrast

Another way that details are arranged in a paragraph is by comparison and contrast. When two things are **compared,** their similarities are discussed. The writer tells you how they are alike and what they have in common. One thing will be said to be equal to another in some way.

This sentence makes a comparison:

The tall bottle holds as much as the short bottle.

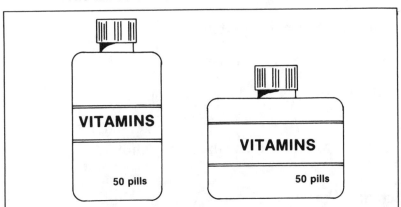

The similarity between the two bottles is in how much you can put in them.

When two things are **contrasted,** their differences are discussed.

This sentence draws a contrast:

The tall bottle costs more than the short bottle.

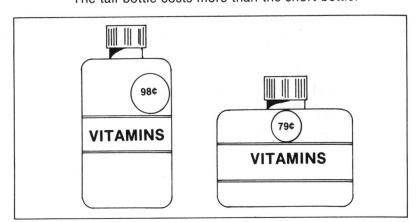

The difference between the bottles (besides how tall they are) is in how much they cost.

There are certain words often used to show comparisons.

similar: Theresa's singing voice is <u>similar</u> to Paulette's.

as...as: He's <u>as</u> tall <u>as</u> Wilt Chamberlain.

like: It's just <u>like</u> you to be late.

the same as: My score was <u>the same as</u> yours.

There are also certain words often used to show contrasts.

on the other hand: I'm very logical. You, <u>on the other hand</u>, are very creative.

—er than: The United Airlines flight was long<u>er than</u> the T.W.A. flight.

Exercise 9

Read the following paragraphs. Underline the words that are used to show comparison or contrast. The first one is done as an example. There are seven more words or word-groups to find. See if you can get them all.

My brother's house is much <u>more modern than</u> my apartment. His electricity bill must be much higher than mine, too. In my apartment only two things are always running: a clock and a refrigerator. In his house, on the other hand, he's got a water-bed heater, the heat for the house, the refrigerator, the computer that controls the electricity, the instant-on TV, a few clocks and the water heater. These are always running.

To me, being there when the dishwasher, microwave oven and power saw were all running was like being on a spaceship. The electricity used by all those devices was great. The computer got as alarmed as the light panel in a spacecraft. A beep-beeping just like the beeping on a modern pinball machine started. Lights blinked like Christmas tree lights. I became as alarmed as the computer and called my brother. He told me not to worry. That was just a signal that the computer would turn off the heat in the house for a while. It would come back on when the electricity demand went down.

Answers start on page 118.

Exercise 10

In the blank by each sentence, write one of these words:
comparison, contrast or neither.
Also, underline the comparing or contrasting words or word groups.

Remember, when two things are **compared**, similarities are shown. When two things are **contrasted**, differences are shown.

1. Those stamps are as scarce as hens' teeth. _____

2. She never enjoyed baby-sitting for sick puppies. _____

3. We have not had nearly as much snow this year as last year. _____

4. How can I prove to you that I know less than you do? _____

5. His eyes were as red as a Texas sunset. _____

6. It's better late than never. _____

7. Jean earns as much as Susan does. _____

8. I am taller than my sister by six inches.
    _____

9. I don't like sitting in the park. _____

10. Her skirt was hot pink. On the other hand, her jacket
    was deep blue. _____

Answers start on page 118.

Seeing Rank of Importance

As a reader one of the things you must see about the
details in a paragraph is which details are most important
and which are not so important. Seeing the **rank of
importance** is like putting "first things first." In newspaper
stories the most important facts or details are almost always
said first. Here's an example:

> The City Council will vote next Tues-
> day. The issues are:
> (1) whether to increase funds for the
> city schools,
> (2) whether to re-name the fire depart-
> ment and
> (3) whether to plant grass or flowers
> around the new pond near the library. After
> the vote, the Council members will picnic in
> Central Park. They want to have a look at
> the new trash cans they voted to buy last
> month. City Council Chairman Bud Miller
> will supply the beer.

Now, that may be carrying it a bit far. But, with each
sentence, the information gets less and less important. (That
is, unless beer is more important than funds for schools.)

All writing is not like newspaper writing, however. Very important and less important things get mixed together. It is the reader's job to decide what is most important.

Here is a paragraph. Each sentence has a blank in front of it. Write numbers in the blanks to show the rank of importance of each sentence. The most important should be number 1.

_____ The Fly-by-Night Airline Company lost a jet in a crash yesterday. _____Three-hundred-and-fifty-four people, who were all headed for Hawaii, were killed. _____ The greeting service in Honolulu had to cancel the cocktail hour planned for the passengers. _____ The airline company has been ordered to cancel all flights until every jet is checked.

How did you rank them? This is a possible order:
1. Three-hundred-and-fifty-four people were killed. (Human life is most important.)

2. The airline had to cancel all flights. (Upsetting other people's plans and losing a lot of money.)

3. A jet was lost. (That probably cost less money than cancelling all flights for a while.)

4. The cocktail party had to be cancelled. (Big deal!)

When you are reading you will understand paragraphs better if you understand cause and effect, comparison and contrast and rank of importance. These are three ways you need to think about the details in a paragraph. Some paragraphs will have cause and effect relationships but no comparisons or contrasts. In some paragraphs the order of importance of the details will be clear. In others the details will be of more equal importance.

PRACTICE

Three reading passages follow. You will be asked questions about each. The questions will be about cause and effect, comparison and contrast and rank of importance. Some questions will ask you to recall details.

Exercise 11

The landlords were happy. The owners of big businesses were happy. The mayor had ordered the closing of one hospital and two schools in a black neighborhood. He said it was to cut spending. The reason he gave for choosing those three places was that they weren't used as much as they once were. He offered landlords and business a big tax break. They would turn the area into middle- and upper-middle-income housing and offices.

The neighborhood residents began picketing the schools, hospitals and the mayor's house, They saw a loss of hundreds of jobs for people in the community. They wondered where their children would go to school. They knew <u>they</u> could not live in the new apartments. The people picketing got angrier as the days went by. The trouble grew until a woman was shot by a policeman. Riots began. They were worse than any riot ever in this city. Twenty-three people were killed; blocks and blocks were burned to the ground; thousands were homeless. In the end, the schools and hospital were closed.

1. The passage (check one)

    _____(1) compares the riot to other riots.

    _____(2) compares the riot to the mayor's order.

    _____(3) contrasts the riot to other riots.

    _____(4) contrasts the riot to the mayor's order.

    _____(5) mentions only one riot.

2. Many things angered the neighborhood about the mayor's order. Name at least three.

(1) _____

_____

_____

(2) _____

_____

_____

(3) _____

_____

_____

3. The mayor used a contrast to explain the order. What was that contrast?

_____(1) He said new houses and offices would look better.

_____(2) He said that the closings would bring better jobs.

_____(3) He said the hospital and schools weren't used as much as they once were.

_____(4) He said middle-income people would be better than the community people.

_____(5) He said the hospital was used as little as the two schools.

4. What was the immediate cause of the riot?

_____(1) The mayor wanted to close one hospital and three schools.

_____(2) A woman was shot by a policeman.

_____(3) People were worried about their children.

_____(4) Twenty-three people were killed.

_____(5) The mayor gave businesses a big tax break.

5. Which of the following was <u>not</u> an effect of the riot?

_____(1) Homes, lives and property were lost.

_____(2) Thousands were made homeless.

_____(3) Blocks were burned to the ground.

_____(4) People were killed; the fighting went on.

_____(5) A woman was shot by a policeman.

Answers start on page 119.

Exercise 12

It seems that when cold weather sets in, city people get more active. In the summer, city people do lazy things. They lie on beaches. They sit and watch ribs barbecue. They watch baseball games. They sip cool drinks. They sit on their steps at night and try to cool off.

When fall comes, they change. All over the city you can see people walking faster. They go to movies, to plays, to concerts. They go disco dancing. People plan more parties in the colder months. They get together more often for dinner, for drinks or to go out.

Perhaps the difference is the greater amount of energy people have when it is cooler.

1. Which two seasons are contrasted in this passage?

_____(1) spring and summer

_____(2) summer and fall

_____(3) fall and winter

_____(4) winter and spring

_____(5) summer and winter

2. In the second paragraph, find the sentence that says, "All over the city you can see people walking faster." That means that they are walking faster than

_____(1) they did in summer.

_____(2) the writer would want them to.

_____(3) other people would walk.

_____(4) they did the year before.

_____(5) they would to go to a disco.

3. Based on what you have read, what seems to be the cause of people doing more when it is cool?

_____(1) There are more things to do.

_____(2) People go back to school and to work.

_____(3) People have more energy when it is cool.

_____(4) People sit on their steps to cool off.

_____(5) People go out more when it is cool.

Answers start on page 120.

Exercise 13

All the widows in the line were dressed in black. They climbed up the steps to the church on their knees. Their heads were bowed like dying flowers. The only sound was the clicking of rosary beads flowing through hundreds of fingers. From far away the line of women looked like a long black snake inching up a rocky hill. Up close, the sound was like a thousand tiny marbles dropping slowly to the floor.

1. The line of women is compared to what?

_____(1) steps

_____(2) a church

_____(3) a sound

_____(4) a snake

_____(5) widows

2. What do the rosary beads sound like?

_____(1) the clicking of hundreds of fingers

_____(2) a long black snake moving

_____(3) a thousand tiny marbles dropping

_____(4) a field of dying flowers

_____(5) people climbing a rocky hill

3. The movement of the widows was

_____(1) very straight and fast.

_____(2) slow but steady.

_____(3) not organized.

_____(4) like dropping slowly to the floor.

_____(5) Nothing in the passage gives a clue.

Answers start on page 120.

REVIEW EXERCISES—HOW DETAILS ARE ARRANGED

Read each of the five passages below and answer the questions.

Review Exercise 1

At 6:30 A.M. on June 11, 1950, Frank Trowbridge was walking his dog. In a vacant lot the dog started barking at a patch of weeds.

Frank went to see what his dog was barking at. He found a body there. It was a girl. She was fully clothed. A crumpled pink rose stuck out from her left hand.

The police put the time of her death at 2:00 A.M. She had been choked to death. She seemed to be about 19 years old. She had no identification. The police called her The Pink Rose.

Detectives found that she had arrived in the city on a Greyhound bus at 10:30 P.M. the night of June 10th.

Mrs. June Jacks recalled talking to the girl on the bus. The girl told Mrs. Jacks her home was in Maine. It was some small town, but Mrs. Jacks couldn't remember the name.

The girl helped Mrs. Jacks off the bus. They both waited 15 minutes to claim their suitcases. The young girl picked up two brown suitcases and left. She walked to the 18th Street entrance. She seemed to be waiting for someone. At 10:55 P.M. Mrs. Jacks got a cab. The girl was still waiting by the curb.

A check of all the cab companies showed no driver had picked up a girl who looked like the Pink Rose between 10:55 P.M. that night and 2:00 A.M. the next day. Police sent pictures of the girl to Maine, but no one knew her. Pictures in the newspaper didn't help either.

Detectives worked on the case for several years with no results. Today, the girl still has no name. She lies in a grave. The only words on the marker are "The Pink Rose, 1950."

What happened to her between 10:55 P.M. and 2:00 A.M.? Who strangled her? After more than 30 years, no one knows.

_____

Look at the times listed as numbers 1 to 7 in the list that follows. Then read the events lettered (a) to (g). Match the event with the time by writing the letter of the event in the space after the time.

1. June 10, 1950 at 10:30 P.M. ____

2. June 10, 1950 at 10:45 P.M. ____

3. June 10, 1950 at 10:55 P.M. ____

4. June 10, 1950 after 10:55 P.M. ____

5. June 10 and 11, 1950 between 10:55 P.M. and 2 A.M. ____

6. June 11, 1950 at 2 A.M. ____

7. June 11, 1950 at 6:30 A.M. ____

(a) Trowbridge finds the girl's body.

(b) the girl arrives in the city.

(c) no cab company picked up the girl as a passenger.

(d) the girl and Mrs. Jacks pick up their bags.

(e) the girl is strangled.

(f) Mrs. Jacks leaves the station in a cab.

(g) the girl is still standing at the curb by the bus station.

Briefly answer the following by filling in the blanks.

8. How was the girl killed? _____

_____

9. In the dead girl's hand was _____

_____

10. Even though her picture was in the papers and sent to Maine, the police were never able to _____

_____

11. The dead girl had lived in _____

_____

12. After more then 30 years, no one has ever _____

Answers start on page 120.

Review Exercise 2

All the saloons in the old wild West had swinging doors. These seemed to be made for drunk troublemakers to come flying through. The troublemakers usually rolled a few times and landed on dusty Main Street.

The one doing the throwing was the saloon's bouncer. Naturally, the bouncer had to be a big, burly, tough man. No puny 150-pounders would make good bouncers.

Gunfights in the saloons were fairly common. So the bouncer had to be a quick-drawer and a good shot too. A bouncer lost only one of these gunfights in his career.

Later, the towns grew, and police departments were started. The saloon bouncers didn't need to carry guns anymore. But better police departments didn't keep the job of bouncing from being a tough one.

In the 1920s drinking was against the law, so illegal bars called speakeasies came into existence. The bouncer couldn't depend on police help for a place that was not legal. He was back to carrying a gun himself and using his fists.

In the 1930s legal bars came back. The bouncer could call on the police for help again. The most trouble arose from drunks starting fights.

Another change appeared in the 1950s. The owners of the bars began to insist on no fights. If they were hurt in a fight, modern customers began to sue the bouncer and the owner.

Nowadays, there are still big tough bouncers in many nightclubs, bars, dance halls and sports arenas. But even the name of "bouncer" is disappearing. The words, "doorman," "crowd moderator" or "I.D. checker" sound much better.

The modern bouncer has a few fights in a year instead of several each night. Some owners even pay a bonus of $25 or more after fights. The bouncer gets the bonus for not punching back at a swinging customer.

Complete the following sentences from this passage by filling in the blanks.

1. In the old wild West many saloons had _____
    _____.

2. _____.
    In those days a bouncer had to be _____,
    _____, and also a _____.

3. When police departments started, bouncers no longer had to _____.

4. During the 1920s bars, sometimes called speakeasies, were _____.

5. The bouncer in a speakeasy could look forward to __
    _____ each night.

6. In the 1930s bars became _____ again.

7. So the bouncer could depend on _____ for help in fights.

8. Later in the 1950s bar owners didn't want bouncers swinging at customers because _____
    _____.

    _____.

9. Some owners even pay bouncers extra for not _____
    _____.

    _____.

10. Now even the name <u>bouncer</u> is disappearing. They are being called _____

    _____.

Answers start on page 121.

Review Exercise 3

Harry Belt had just bought a brand new refrigerator-freezer for his wife. He had it for less than a month when trouble came.

The trouble didn't come from the refrigerator-freezer itself. The problem came from the electric power company. One day they completely shut off Harry's electricity. The company claimed that Harry hadn't paid his electricity bill.

Harry and his wife came home from work that evening. There was water all over the floor and on the carpet. The food in the refrigerator was ruined.

Harry figured that the damage was $250. The electric company had shut off the wrong person's electricity. Harry had paid his bill. But they refused to do anything about it.

For several months Harry tried to collect $250 from the company. It was still no use; they wouldn't pay.

Harry couldn't afford a lawyer to take the company to court. So was he stuck then for the $250?

No, not necessarily. Every state has a small claims court. All citizens can use this court to get back small amounts of money. In some states the claims can be no larger than $500. Other states will allow you to sue for $1,000 in a small claims court.

All Harry had to do was to go to his nearest small claims court. He could file a suit there. The court would charge him $3 to $10, depending on what state he lives in.

The clerk of the court would advise Harry about his chances of winning his case. Then the clerk would set a trial date. Then Harry could be his own lawyer.

There is no guarantee that you will win your case. Harry did. He got back all damages, including his court filing fee and lost wages from work.

Small claims court is something to keep in mind.

The 12 events below are from the passage, but they are mixed up. Try to figure out the order in which the events should come. Start with the earliest and go to the latest. Write the letter of the first event by number 1; the second, by number 2; the third, by number 3 and so on.

1.____ (a) Harry became his own lawyer.

2.____ (b) Water ruined the Belts' floor and carpet.

3.____ (c) The electric power company refused to pay damages.

4.____ (d) Harry bought a new refrigerator-freezer for his wife.

5.____ (e) Harry couldn't afford to hire a lawyer.

6.____ (f) Harry files a claim in small claims court.

7.____ (g) The power company turned off the wrong person's electricity.

8.____ (h) Harry and his wife discover the mess after work one evening.

9.____ (i) Harry wasn't sure he could win the case.

10.____ (j) Harry pays a small fee to file his claim in court.

11.____ (k) The power company had to pay all the damages.

12.____ (l) A clerk advises Harry as to whether he can win or not.

Answers start on page 122.

Review Exercise 4

Baths and bathing haven't always been what they are today. Perhaps today the average person who lives in the United States takes a bath or shower every day. Daily bathing, or even bathing every other day, is something new.

The earliest mention of bathing in the Bible is in the

Old Testament. Bathing is not mentioned there as a way to get clean, though. Bathing is part of a religious practice.

In more recent centuries people have known about the medical importance of different types of baths. They have used natural hot baths, bubbling baths and salt water baths in strange-smelling natural waters. Each type has been thought to have a special effect: some for muscle pain, some for tension, etc.

It was not until rather recently that baths were considered an important part of cleanliness. For a long time people didn't know about germs. So, why wash? Even 70 to 80 years ago, the Saturday night bath was a real thing. It was the only bath of the week. That's even better than in the 1400s. Then, in England, baths came once a year. Queen Elizabeth I was no rose! Now most people bathe daily because it is known to be important for good health.

Answer each question according to directions.

1. Put numbers in the blanks by each sentence to show the chronological order (time order) of events. Number 1 will be the thing that came first.

_____Daily bathing became common.

_____Baths were known to have medical importance, such as relieving tension.

_____Baths came once a year.

_____Baths were part of a religious practice.

_____Baths were taken once a week.

2. Which is the least important sentence in the last paragraph? (The paragraph doesn't even need the sentence to get its point across.) Copy the sentence.

Answer:_____

3. What is one reason that people started bathing more often in the last few years? Check the correct answer.

_____(1) The bathtub was invented.

_____(2) People had learned about germs.

_____(3) People found out that bathing would relieve tension.

_____(4) People couldn't stand the smell of each other anymore.

_____(5) People's work became dirtier after machinery was invented. They had to bathe more.

ANSWERS AND EXPLANATIONS—HOW DETAILS ARE ARRANGED

Exercise 1

1. In the 1950s nearly 100 atomic bombs were dropped in Nevada.
2. Each of the 1,000 has been affected by medical problems.
3. They believe the radiation from the bombs caused their illnesses.
4. Nearly 1,000 people in Nevada began to sue the government in the 1970s.

Exercise 2

1. He had lived in the country before his mother died.
2. After his mother died, Vanka became the servant of a shoemaker in the city.
3. As was common, he was beaten, starved and given too much work to do.
4. He had bought the envelope the day before and hidden it.
5. Vanka wrote a letter to his grandfather one Christmas.
6. When he finished the letter, he sealed it in an envelope.
7. On the outside he wrote his grandfather's name —nothing more.
8. He dropped it in a mailbox in the middle of Moscow.
9. He went to bed happy.
10. In the 1800s Anton Chekhov wrote a true story about a 9-year-old boy named Vanka.

Exercise 3

There is more than one way you could have put the story in order by time. Here's just one way. If you found another way, go over it with a friend.

1. (f) Her mother helped her get dressed.
2. (g) They couldn't find the veil.
3. (e) I helped her put on her flowers.
4. (d) When Charlotte was coming down the aisle, everyone looked pleased.
5. (i) The groom was so nervous he couldn't find the ring.
6. (j) The preacher had to slap him in the face to calm him down.
7. (a) The first thing I did was eat three shrimp cocktails.
8. (b) Your Uncle Bob Junior got there.
9. (c) I saw him put some shrimp in his suitcase.
10. (h) When the cake was cut, the lights went out for a minute.
11. (l) Someone had taken the first slice of cake.
12. (k) When the lights came on. . . .

Exercise 4

1. (a) A church service in Indianapolis, Indiana was ended by a woman.
    (b) The invaders first landed in Grover's Mill, New Jersey.
    (c) Viking spaceships have landed on the planet Mars.
    (d) A woman in Pittsburgh, Pennsylvania threatened to take poison.
    (e) The play was broadcast from New York City.

Your answers may be slightly different. The ideas should be similar to those answers.

2. (a) Orson Welles was <u>the actor who put on the radio play "War of the Worlds."</u>

(b) Welles was very surprised because <u>he didn't know anyone would think the play was real.</u>

(c) Many thousands thought the play was <u>real.</u>

(d) The play was broadcast on the <u>radio on Halloween.</u>

(e) It did no good, but the police tried to <u>tell people that the play (or broadcast) was not real.</u>

Exercise 5

1. Max Anderson had to <u>rent or borrow</u> his first horse from a stable. A worker there had to tell Max not to <u>get on the horse from the wrong side.</u>

In the first scene of the movie called "<u>The Great Train Robbery</u>" the horse <u>bucked</u> Max off. So Max had to become a <u>bandit or robber</u> on foot. This was a poor start, but Max still became the movies' first <u>cowboy or Western star.</u>

2. (a) <u>Women:</u> Cowboys never kissed, married or fell in love with them.

(b) <u>Fighting:</u> The cowboy never fought or used violence unless in self-defense.

(c) <u>Horses:</u> The cowboy had to be a good rider, able to do tricks of all kinds on a horse.

(d) <u>Guns:</u> The cowboy had to be an excellent shot.

Exercise 6

1. (d) He is born in Mobile, Alabama in 1906.
2. (c) Satchel throws rocks because he is too poor to own a real baseball.
3. (e) Satchel gets his nickname from carrying suitcases at a train station.
4. (g) He begins hanging around local ball fields and getting into games.
5. (b) Satchel goes to reform school for taking some toys.
6. (h) He becomes a pro player and pitches in Negro leagues.
7. (j) Satchel often hears big league stars tell him, "If you were only white!"
8. (i) The major leagues drop color rules against blacks after World War II.
9. (a) Satchel shuts out the Chicago White Sox in his first game in Cleveland, Ohio.
10. (f) Satchel was still pitching in the majors in his fifties.

Exercise 7

1. <u>Because</u> Congress cut spending on job programs, many people still have no work.

Or

Many people still have no work <u>because</u> Congress cut spending on job programs.

Cause: Congress cut spending on job programs.

Effect: Many people still have no work.

2. <u>Because</u> some religions say that men can have many wives, they marry two or more.

Or

Some men marry two or more wives <u>because</u> their religions say that they can.

    Cause: Some religions say that men can have many wives.

    Effect: Men marry two or more wives.

3. <u>Because</u> they studied, they did well on the test.

Or

They did well on the test <u>because</u> they studied.

    Cause: They studied.

    Effect: They did well on the test.

4. <u>Because</u> Ned stuck it with a pin, the balloon burst.

Or

The balloon burst <u>because</u> Ned stuck it with a pin.

    Cause: Ned stuck the balloon with a pin.

    Effect: The balloon burst.

5. <u>Because</u> she stopped eating meat, Agnes lost 15 pounds.

Or

Agnes lost 15 pounds <u>because</u> she stopped eating meat.

    Cause: Agnes stopped eating meat.

    Effect: Agnes lost 15 pounds.

Exercise 8

There are four cause and effect relationships in the story. You should have written down three of these:

1. Cause: A candle fell over.
    Effect: The house caught fire.
2. Cause: Flames from the burning house jumped to the barn.
    Effect: The flames caught the barn on fire.
3. Cause: Fire in the barn scared the horses.
    Effect: The horses ran out of the barn.
4. Cause: The horses ran over the dog.
    Effect: The dog died.

There is one more cause and effect relationship not exactly stated in the story. It would be a good answer, too.

5. Cause: The farmer's wife died.

    Effect: They put her in a casket and put candles around it.

Exercise 9

My brother's house is much <u>more modern than</u> my apartment. His electricity bill must be much <u>higher than</u> mine, too. In my apartment, only two things are always running: a clock and a refrigerator. In his house, <u>on the other hand</u>, he's got a water-bed heater, the heat for the house, the refrigerator, the computer that controls the electricity, the instant-on T.V., a few clocks and the water heater. These are always running.

To me, being there when the dishwasher, microwave oven and power saw were all running was <u>like</u> being on a spaceship. The electricity used by all those devices was great. The computer got <u>as alarmed as</u> the light panel in a spacecraft. A beep-beeping <u>just like</u> the beeping on a modern pinball machine started. Lights blinked <u>like</u> Christmas tree lights. I became <u>as alarmed as</u> the computer and called my brother. He told me not to worry. That was just a signal that the computer would turn off the heat in the house for a while. It would come back on when the electricity demand went down.

Exercise 10

1. Comparison. <u>as . . . as</u>. Stamps and teeth are equally scarce. They compare.

2. Neither. No comparison or contrast is made.

3. Contrast. <u>not . . . as . . . as</u>. The amounts of snow differ. They contrast.

4. Contrast. <u>less than</u>. We don't know the same amount. We contrast.

5. Comparison. <u>as . . . as</u>. Eyes and sunset are equally red. They compare.

6. Contrast. <u>better . . . than</u>. Late and never are not equally good. They contrast.

7. Comparison. <u>as . . . as</u>. The two women earn the same amount. They compare.

8. Contrast. <u>taller than</u>. We aren't the same height. We contrast.

9. Neither. No comparison or contrast is made.

10. Contrast. <u>On the other hand</u>. Her shirt and jacket were different colors. They contrast.

Exercise 11

1. (3) The passage says the riot was worse than any in the city, ever. It was more serious than all earlier riots.

2. (1) Two schools would be closed.
   (2) A hospital would be closed.
   (3) Landlords would get a tax break to build middle- and upper-middle income housing. The neighborhood people couldn't live in the housing.
   (4) People would lose jobs.
   (5) The children would lose their schools.

3. (3) The mayor drew this contrast: He said the schools and hospital were not used <u>as</u> much <u>as</u> they once were.

4. (2) A woman was shot by a policeman.

5. (5) A woman being shot was one of the <u>causes</u> of the riot.

Exercise 12

1. (2) summer and fall; the first paragraph has the words, "In the summer . . . ." The second paragraph has the words, "When fall comes . . . ."
2. (1) they did in summer; the first paragraph talks about how slow and lazy people feel in summer. The second talks about the same people in fall. The people are contrasted with themselves at the two different times of the year.
3. (3) People have more energy when it is cool. The last paragraph says people have a "greater amount of energy" when it is cooler.

Exercise 13

1. (4) a snake; the passage says that from a distance they looked like a long black snake.
2. (3) a thousand tiny marbles dropping; the last sentence of the paragraph says this.
3. (2) slow but steady; the line of women looked like ". . . a snake inching up a rocky hill." Inching means moving slowly but steadily.

ANSWERS AND EXPLANATIONS—REVIEW EXERCISES

Review Exercise 1

1. (b) The girl arrives in the city.
2. (d) The girl and Mrs. Jacks pick up their bags.
3. (f) Mrs. Jacks leaves the station in a cab.

4. (g) The girl is still standing at the curb by the bus station.

5. (c) No cab company picked up the girl as a passenger.

6. (e) The girl is strangled.

7. (a) Trowbridge finds the girl's body.

8. She was strangled <u>or</u> choked to death.

9. a pink rose.

10. find anyone who knew her.

11. a small town in Maine.

12. found out who she was or who killed her.

Review Exercise 2

1. In the old wild West many saloons had <u>swinging doors</u>.

2. In those days a bouncer had to be <u>big, burly, tough</u> and also a <u>good shot</u>.

3. When police departments became better, bouncers no longer had to <u>carry guns</u>.

4. During the 1920s bars, sometimes called speakeasies, were <u>not legal (illegal)</u>.

5. The bouncer in a speakeasy could look forward to <u>several fights</u> each night.

6. In the 1930s bars became <u>legal</u> again.

7. So the bouncer could depend on <u>the police</u> for help in fights.

8. Later in the 1950s, bar owners didn't want bouncers swinging at customers because <u>the customers would get hurt and sue</u>.

9. Some owners even pay bouncers extra for not <u>swinging back at customers in fights</u>.

10. Now even the name bouncer is disappearing. They are

being called <u>I.D. checkers, doormen, crowd moderators.</u>

Review Exercise 3

1. (d) Harry bought a new refrigerator-freezer for his wife.
2. (g) The power company turned off the wrong person's electricity.
3. (b) Water ruined the Belts' floor and carpet.
4. (h) Harry and his wife discover the mess after work one evening.
5. (c) The electric power company refused to pay damages.
6. (e) Harry couldn't afford to hire a lawyer.
7. (i) Harry wasn't sure he could win the case.
8. (l) A clerk advises Harry as to whether he can win or not.
9. (j) Harry pays a small fee to file his claim in court.
10. (f) Harry files a claim in small claims court.
11. (a) Harry became his own lawyer.
12. (k) The power company had to pay all the damages.

Review Exercise 4

1. (1) Baths were part of religious practice.
   (2) Baths came once a year.
   (3) Baths were known to have medical importance, such as relieving tension.
   (4) Baths were taken once a week.
   (5) Daily bathing became common.
2. So, why wash?
3. (2) People had learned about germs.

3 LEARNING NEW WORDS WHEN READING

There are many ways to figure out the meaning of new words while you are reading. In the long run, the best way to find out the meaning of a word is to look it up in a dictionary. But sometimes that isn't possible. This unit will show you some ways to figure out the meaning of a new word as you're reading.

The first way to figure out the meaning of a word is from its context. The **context** is the other words and sentences that are around the new word. When you figure out the meaning of a word from context you are making a guess about what the word means. To do this you use the hints and clues of the other words and sentences. You won't always be right, but many times you will be. You might not be able to guess the exact meaning of a word, but you may be close enough to get the meaning of the sentence it is in.

USING CONTEXT TO LEARN NEW WORDS

Imagine the word thwart on a piece of blank paper all by itself with no sentences or paragraphs with it. Thwart on this paper has no context. It's all alone. You would have a hard time guessing the meaning of thwart because it has no context.

Read this story with thwart in it. See if you can make a guess at its meaning.

> Last night in New York's Madison
> Square Garden, Jerry Robins knocked out
> Eddie "Killer" Kain in the third round of
> their middleweight fight. Robins hit Kain

with two solid left hooks and a hard right uppercut.

Killer Kain had to be carried from the ring on a stretcher. He was reported in fair condition at St. Luke's Hospital.

This knockout will probably thwart Killer Kain's try to win back the championship he lost last spring. He may be forced to quit the ring.

Now can you guess at the meaning of thwart?

Write your guess in this space:

To thwart means to _____

If you wrote something like "stop" or "keep from," you're right.

Exercise 1

Below are four paragraphs. Try to guess the meaning of the underlined word in each paragraph from its context. Write your guess in the space after the paragraph.

1. The police pulled a car over to the curb. They saw the driver quickly conceal something under his coat. They made the driver lean up against the hood of his car. They wanted to find what he had concealed under his coat.
   Conceal: _____

2. A cigarette ash fell into a stack of newspapers. A fire started. The young boy at the table grabbed a half gallon of milk. He threw it onto the blaze. The milk extinguished the fire completely before it could spread very far.
   Extinguish: _____

3. The wind blew 50 miles an hour at the men. The snow blinded them and the cold numbed them. They were trying to reach the car which was already half buried in a snowdrift. All of these—the snow, the wind and the cold—hampered their attempts to pull the car from the drift.

Hamper: _____

4. Can you really domesticate a wild animal? Many experts say no, not even if you raise the animal from birth. Lions or tigers domesticated from birth will often, without warning, go wild. For no reason, they will attack those who have raised them. Even normal domesticated animals like dogs sometimes go wild and attack without reason.

Domesticated: _____

Answers start on page 144.

USING SYNONYMS AND ANTONYMS

One way to figure out a word's meaning from its context is to look for other words nearby that seem to mean the same thing as the word you don't know. Here's an example:

Mrs. Beek was a very strict teacher. In class she wouldn't put up with students whispering, talking out of turn or passing notes. Of course, she absolutely wouldn't tolerate eating candy or chewing gum in her classroom.

Can you tell from the context what tolerate means?

Tolerate: _____

What other words in the paragraph mean the same thing as tolerate?

_____

Put up with means the same as tolerate. A strict teacher won't put up with whispering or eating in class. A strict teacher won't tolerate these things. Two words that mean the same thing are called **synonyms**. A synonym for *fast* is *quick*. *Stop, quit* and *cease* are all synonyms.

Sometimes there is another word in the context that means the opposite of a word you don't know. Can you tell what the underlined word in this sentence means?

The basketball player looked gigantic as he stood next to his tiny wife.

Gigantic: _____

Which word in the sentence means the opposite of gigantic?

_____

Did you figure out that tiny means the opposite of gigantic? Gigantic means huge or very large. Gigantic and tiny are **antonyms**. They have opposite meanings. Some other antonyms are *hot* and *cold, soft* and *hard* and *wet* and *dry*.

In these next exercises look for synonyms and antonyms to help you find the meaning of the underlined word from its context.

Exercise 2

After each paragraph fill in the blank with the meaning of the underlined word. Then circle the word or words in the paragraph that means the same as or the opposite of the underlined word.

1. Suppose a person earns $120 a week at a job. We all know he isn't going to get the whole $120. Some taxes are deducted. Social Security Tax, State Income Tax and Federal Income Tax are the main taxes taken out of everyone's check.
    Deduct: _____

2. It's ridiculous for you to carry all those bags alone. It was crazy for you to think you could take them home all by yourself.
    Ridiculous: _____

3. When we grew up in that small town, we trusted everyone. Now we are suspicious. We don't like to open our door to strangers.
    Suspicious: _____

4. Tom's life has been tragic. His wife was killed in a car crash. His son died of cancer. On the other hand, his sister Meg has had a happy life. She has a husband and children that she loves. She has plenty of money.
    Tragic: _____

Answers start on page 144.

USING EXAMPLES AND DESCRIPTIONS

Sometimes you can figure out the meaning of a word by finding examples or descriptions in the context of what that word means. Can you figure out the meaning of the underlined word in this paragraph?

Jack was very aggressive. He was always pushing people around or getting into fights. He was most aggressive when he drank too much. If he went into a bar you could expect some trouble.

Aggressive: _____

You could probably tell that aggressive means pushy and ready to attack because the other sentences describe how Jack is always getting into fights. Here's another one:

Grandma doesn't like contemporary music. She doesn't like Stevie Wonder, Aretha Franklin, Donna Summer or any disco music. She only listens to her old Billie Holiday records.

Contemporary: _____

Stevie Wonder, Donna Summer and Aretha Franklin are all singers who are living and singing right now. That is what contemporary means: something that is happening today.

Exercise 3

Here are four exercises with words to figure out from the context. Write the meaning of the underlined word in the blank.

1. The group had played for two hours. There were 5,000 teenagers there listening to their favorite rock-and-roll band. The audience was clapping, screaming and cheering. After the show was over they applauded for fifteen minutes, so the band came back to play another song.
    Applaud: _____

2. Jim enjoys many kinds of recreation. He plays football in the fall and basketball in the winter. He also likes some quiet forms of recreation like reading books and playing his guitar.

Recreation: _____

3. Several factors contributed to the car crash. First, the road was icy. It was a winding road with many twists and turns. Also the driver was very tired. He had been driving all night. If it hadn't been for these factors, perhaps there wouldn't have been an accident.

Factor: _____

4. My little brother Tim was blowing up a balloon. The more he blew, the more the balloon expanded. It got bigger and bigger. I told him to stop or it would break. But he didn't listen. The balloon expanded until it burst. Tim cried and screamed because his balloon was gone.

Expand: _____

Answers start on page 145.

USING WORD PARTS

Read the following passage. See if you can use its context to figure out the word misanthrope.

My grandfather hadn't spoken to anyone for years. He lived in his big old house with four cats. Grandma had died 20 years ago. He had pictures of her all over the house. He was very deaf. He could hardly hear at all. I think he spent the days talking to his pictures of Grandma. If the doorbell rang, he wouldn't even answer it. People thought my grandfather was a misanthrope.

Can you guess what <u>misanthrope</u> means? Does it mean someone who is old and alone? Or does it mean a man who misses his dead wife? Maybe it is someone who wants to be left alone. It might even be a person who has some disease or someone who loves cats. From this context you can't be sure what <u>misanthrope</u> means.

If you can't figure out the meaning of a word from context, you may have to look it up in a dictionary. But there is one other thing you can try first. You can check to see if you know what a part of the word means. Perhaps you have heard of *anthropology*. *Anthropology* is the study of people and culture. The beginning of the word *anthropology* is the same as the ending of the word <u>misanthrope</u>. Both of these words have **-anthrop-** in them. The word-part **anthrop-** always has something to do with people or mankind. Now, what about **mis-**? Can you think of other words that begin with **mis-**? Write three here:

_____   _____   _____

There are many words that begin with **mis-**. You might have written down *mistake, misspell* or *mistreat*. What do all of these words have in common? All of them mean that something is done wrong or badly. A *misspelled* word is a word that is spelled wrong. If you *mistreat* someone, you treat them badly. If someone *mistrusts* you, they don't think you should be trusted. A <u>misanthrope</u> is someone who hates people. If you can figure out what the two parts of <u>misan-thrope</u> mean, you might be able to guess what the whole word means.

Many words can be broken down into two or three parts. If you know what the parts mean, you may be able to guess what the meaning of the whole word is.

Root Words

The most basic part of a word is its **root**. All words have roots. Parts may be added to the word before or after the root. Or a word may be just a root with nothing added. *Blue* is a word that is just a root word with nothing added. So is *sad*. *Move, talk, leg, put* and *stand* are all root words with nothing added.

Prefixes

Remove is a root word with a prefix added. A **prefix** is a word part that comes before the root. Can you think of some other words that have the same prefix as *remove*? Write three of them here:

_____ _____ _____

The prefix **re-** is part of many words. Some of the words you might have written are *recall, remember, remake, resell, research, repeat, rebound, rebirth, reverse* and *review*. The prefix **re-** means to do something over again. When you *remember* something, you think of it again. When you *review* something, you look at it again. To *repeat* is to say something over again. A *rebound* in basketball is getting the ball back again. The root of *remake* is *make*. To *remake* something is to make it over again. The root of *rebirth* is *birth*. To be *reborn* is to be born again after some important experience in your life.

Another common prefix is **un-**. *Unhappy, unhelpful, uncomfortable, unfortunate, unbroken* and *undone* all have the prefix **un-**. Can you guess what this prefix means? Write your answer here:

Someone who is *unhappy* is not happy. If you have left your job of cutting the grass *undone*, you haven't cut the grass. The only *unbroken* toy in the toybox is the one toy that is not broken. The prefix **un-** means not.

Exercise 4

Below are three lists of words. The words in each list have the same prefix. For each list draw a line under the prefix. Write what you think the prefix means. Look at the root words, but write the meaning of the whole word in the space.

1. (a) dishonest _____
    (b) disagree _____
    (c) disable _____
    (d) disinfect _____
    (e) dislike _____
Prefix meaning: _____

2. (a) invisible _____
    (b) indecent _____
    (c) indistinct _____
    (d) ineffective _____
    (e) inexperienced _____
Prefix meaning: _____

3. (a) antifreeze _____
    (b) antiperspirant _____
    (c) antipoverty _____
    (d) antidote _____
    (e) antiracism _____
Prefix meaning: _____

Answers start on page 145.

Suffixes

A **suffix** is a word part that comes <u>after</u> the root. The suffix is always the last part of a word. *Occupant* is a word with a suffix. You may sometimes get mail addressed to "Occupant." An *occupant* is a person who occupies a certain space. The root of *occupant* is *occupy*. An **-ant** or **-ent** added to the end of a word means the person who does what the root word says. An *occupant* is a person who occupies a place. A *resident* is a person who resides somewhere. A *respondent* is someone who responds to some question.

Another common suffix is **-er** or **-or**. *Teacher, visitor, worker, farmer* and *maker* are all words that have this suffix. Can you guess what the **-er** and **-or** suffixes mean? Write your guess here:

_____

The **er** and **or** suffix is similar to the **-ant** and **-ent** suffix. They both mean that a person does what the root word says. A teacher is a person who teaches. A visitor is someone who pays a visit. A farmer is someone who farms the land.

Many words have the suffix **-ful**. Can you list three words with this ending?

_____   _____   _____

Some of the words you might have included in your list are *helpful, fearful, careful, restful, joyful* and *useful*. This suffix means full of. If you are *joyful* you are full of joy. A tool that is *useful* has many different uses.

Exercise 5

Below are three lists of words. The words in each list have the same suffix. For each list, draw a line under the suffix. Write what you think the suffix means. Then, look at the root words, but write the meaning of the whole word in the space.

1. (a) heartless:_____

    (b) painless:_____

    (c) pointless:_____

    (d) shoeless:_____

    (e) friendless:_____

Suffix meaning_____

2. (a) biggest:_____

    (b) hardest:_____

    (c) loudest:_____

    (d) sweetest:_____

    (e) oldest:_____

Suffix meaning_____

3. (a) bakery:_____

    (b) nursery:_____

    (c) cannery:_____

    (d) grocery:_____

    (e) fishery:_____

Suffix Meaning:_____

Answers start on page 146.

LOOKING AT COMPOUND WORDS

If you can't figure out the meaning of a word from context and you don't recognize its prefixes and suffixes, there is one more way you can try to guess its meaning. Some words are made up of two words put together. If you see an unfamiliar word, you should see if it will break down into two words that you do know.

A **compound word** is a word that is made up of two other words. Sometimes you will know the meanings of the two words that make up the compound word. By thinking of the two words together you will sometimes get the meaning of the compound word. *Lawnmower* is a word like this. So are *haircut* and *softball*. Breaking these words down into two words will tell you what the meaning of the compound word is.

In other cases the two words you get by breaking down the compound word will not help you. *Radioactive* is this kind of word. You probably know the words *radio* and *active,* but that doesn't explain what *radioactive* means. However, you may have heard the word *radioactive* before. Maybe you just didn't recognize it when you saw it written down. In this case breaking down the compound word still helped you.

Exercise 6

On the following page are two columns of words. Find a word from column B that can be added to the word from column A to make a compound word. Write the new compound word in the blank.

	A	**B**
1.	rip_____	side
2.	brain_____	off
3.	hill_____	throat
4.	battle_____	man
5.	cut_____	field
6.	short_____	guard
7.	pig_____	pen
8.	safe_____	port
9.	watch_____	wash
10.	pass_____	cut

Answers start on page 147.

Exercise 7

Below is a list of words with blanks before them. Put another word in the blank to form a compound word. For every word listed there are several blanks. Make a different compound word for each. There are several correct answers for each word.

1. (a) _____body
   (b) _____body
   (c) _____body

2. (a) _____man
   (b) _____man
   (c) _____man

3. (a) _____where
   (b) _____where
   (c) _____where

Answers start on page 147.

Exercise 8

Here is a list of eight compound words. Below the list is a list of hints about their meanings. In the blank in front of each meaning, write the compound word that matches the meaning.

blacktop   fingerprints
freeloader   spotlight
bedridden   lawnmower
rainbow   paperback

1. _____ : a kind of covering used on roads and streets

2. _____ : a colorful arch in the sky after a rainstorm

3. _____ : a person who wants something for nothing

4. _____ : we all have these; nobody's are like anyone else's

5. _____ : a machine used to cut grass

6. _____ : a book with a soft cover

7. _____ : a bright beam of light that shines on one certain place

8. _____ : having to stay in bed for long periods of time

Answers start on page 148.

Exercise 9

In the following sentences look at the underlined compound words. Break them into their parts and write each part on the lines. On the other lines write the meaning of the word.

Example: The rock smashed the <u>windshield</u> of the motorcycle.

1st Part: _wind_

2nd Part: _shield_

Meaning: _a plastic or glass cover to protect_
the rider from wind, rocks and bugs

1. All the <u>rubbernecks</u> at the accident got in the way of the ambulance and the police.

    1st Part:_____

    2nd Part:_____

    Meaning:_____

2. The workmen used a <u>cherrypicker</u> to change the burned out streetlights.

    1st Part:_____

    2nd Part:_____

    Meaning:_____

3. The championship game was a complete <u>sellout</u> for a month in advance.

    1st Part:_____

2nd Part:_____

Meaning:_____

4. Mrs. Cumins pointed out all her husband's <u>shortcomings</u>
    to the whole neighborhood.
    1st Part:_____
    2nd Part:_____
    Meaning:_____

5. The player brought a million dollar <u>lawsuit</u> against the
    team for his injuries.
    1st Part:_____
    2nd Part:_____
    Meaning:_____

6. When he became excited, Bill was very <u>scatterbrained</u>
    about remembering anything.
    1st Part:_____
    2nd Part:_____
    Meaning:_____

Answers start on page 148.

In this unit we have worked with many ways to figure
out words when you are reading. By looking at the context
of a word and at its different parts, you can often guess the
meaning. It's a good habit to write the word down. When
you're through reading, you can look it up in the dictionary.
This will give you a more exact meaning and will explain
more completely what the word means.

REVIEW EXERCISES—LEARNING NEW WORDS WHEN READING

Review Exercise 1

Three common suffixes are **-less, -ful** and **-ness.** Below is a list of six root words. Decide which suffix can be used to make a new word. Write the new word in the space. For some of the words, there may be more than one possible answer. You may need to check the new words with a friend or in a dictionary. Watch your spelling.

1. happy _____(change the <u>y</u> to <u>i</u>.)

2. mind _____

3. harm _____

4. sweet _____

5. power _____

6. busy _____(change the <u>y</u> to <u>i</u>.)

7. need _____

8. joy _____

9. care _____

10. beauty _____(change the <u>y</u> to <u>i</u>.)

Answers start on page 149.

Review Exercise 2

Three common prefixes are **super-, over-** and **semi-.** Below is a list of root words. Decide which prefix can be used to make a new word. Write the new word in the space. You may need to check your new words with a friend or in a dictionary.

1. _____man

2. _____cook

3. _____dry

4. _____paid

5. _____sweet

6. _____power

7. _____bearing

8. _____market

9. _____circle

10. _____done

11. _____final

12. _____star

13. _____land

14. _____natural

15. _____night

Answers start on page 150.

Review Exercise 3

Make compound words from the two lists below. Find the word from list B that can go with the word from list A. You may use some words from list B more than once. You may need to read the new words to a friend or check them in a dictionary.

A		B
1. flash	_____	shop
2. work	_____	net
3. full	_____	out
4. fish	_____	come
5. black	_____	cycle
6. fire	_____	hole
7. over	_____	light
8. motor	_____	coat
9. out	_____	place
10. loop	_____	back

Answers start on page 150.

Review Exercise 4

Below is a list of compound words. These are followed by five hints. Write the compound word in the space next to the hint it belongs to. Check your answers.

hairpin
warehouse
headline
loudmouth
sunset

1. A word for the sun going down in the west at evening:_____

2. A type of sharp curve on mountain roads, but also something used by women:_____

3. A person who is always talking and not very quietly:

   _____

4. A building for storing all kinds of goods:

   _____

5. The big print that is put above a newspaper story:

   _____

ANSWERS AND EXPLANATIONS—LEARNING NEW WORDS WHEN READING

Exercise 1

Don't worry if the meanings you wrote down are not exactly the answer given here. It is important that you get the general idea of the word.

1. Conceal: to hide; to cover up
2. Extinguish: to put out
3. Hamper: to make difficult; to slow down; to hold back; to keep from doing quickly
4. Domesticate: to tame; to make a pet of

Exercise 2

Count your answer correct if you had the right idea. Don't worry if your words weren't exactly the same as the answers here.

1. Deduct: to take away; to take out of
    You should have circled the words taken out of.

2. Ridiculous: crazy; silly; senseless
    You should have circled crazy.

3. Suspicious: thinking someone is going to hurt you; not trusting someone
    You should have circled trusted.

4. Tragic: unhappy; full of sadness and misfortune; very bad
    You should have circled happy.

Exercise 3

Count your answer correct if you had the right idea. Don't worry if your words weren't exactly the same as the answers here.

1. Applaud: to clap your hands to show enjoyment of something
2. Recreation: spare-time activities; hobbies; sports; fun
3. Factor: reasons; causes; some events that lead to other events
4. Expand: to get bigger; to get larger

Exercise 4

Your answers may be slightly different.

1. Prefix meaning: **dis-** means not; the loss of; to take away.
    (a) dishonest: not honest; not fair
    (b) disagree: to differ in opinion; not to agree
    (c) disable: to take away ability to do something
    (d) disinfect: to take away germs that cause disease
    (e) dislike: a feeling of not liking

2. Prefix meaning: **in-** means **not**.
    (a) invisible: not visible; not able to be seen
    (b) indecent: not decent; not proper
    (c) indistinct: not distinct; not easy to hear, see or understand; not clear
    (d) ineffective: not effective; not able to make something happen; without power
    (e) inexperienced: not experienced; without knowledge or skill in an area

3. Prefix meaning: **anti** means against or opposed to.
   (a) <u>anti</u>freeze: a protection against freezing; a liquid added to something else to keep it from freezing
   (b) <u>anti</u>perspirant: an item used to stop perspiration or sweat
   (c) <u>anti</u>poverty: something or someone who is opposed to poverty; who fights against it or tries to change it.
   (d) <u>anti</u>dote: a medicine that works against a poison
   (e) <u>anti</u>racism: a feeling or attitude that is against racism

Exercise 5

Your answers might be slightly different.

1. Suffix meaning: **–less** means without or not having.
   (a) heart<u>less</u>: without a heart; mean, cold or cruel
   (b) pain<u>less</u>: without pain; something that does not hurt
   (c) point<u>less</u>: without a point; not having a point; not making sense
   (d) shoe<u>less</u>: without shoes; not having shoes; barefoot
   (e) friend<u>less</u>: without friends; alone

2. Suffix meaning: **–est** means most.
   (a) bigg<u>est</u>: the one that is the most big
   (b) hard<u>est</u>: the one that is the most hard
   (c) loud<u>est</u>: the one that is the most loud
   (d) sweet<u>est</u>: the one that is the most sweet
   (e) old<u>est</u>: the one that is the most old

3. Suffix meaning: **-ery** means a place where something is done.

    (a) bak<u>ery</u>: a place where bread, cakes, pies, cookies and other things are baked

    (b) nurs<u>ery</u>: a place where small children, animals or plants are cared for

    (c) cann<u>ery</u>: a place where food is canned

    (d) groc<u>ery</u>: a place where food and household items are sold

    (e) fish<u>ery</u>: a place where fish are raised

Exercise 6

1. ripoff
2. brainwash
3. hillside
4. battlefield
5. cutthroat
6. shortcut
7. pigpen
8. safeguard
9. watchman
10. passport

Exercise 7

1. Any of these words could have been used.

    anybody   everybody

    nobody   somebody

2. Any of these words could have been used. There are others, too.

watchman   fireman   mailman

policeman   deliveryman   foreman

3. Any of these words could have been used.

somewhere   everywhere

anywhere   nowhere

You may have made other words that are correct for this exercise. If your word isn't listed here, check in a dictionary to be sure it is correct.

Exercise 8

1. blacktop
2. rainbow
3. freeloader
4. fingerprints
5. lawnmower
6. paperback
7. spotlight
8. bedridden

Exercise 9

1. 1st Part: rubber
   2nd Part: necks
   Meaning: people who are turning their heads to watch the accident

2. 1st Part: cherry

   2nd Part: picker

   Meaning: an electric bucket on the back of a truck that lifts the worker right up to the light

3. 1st Part: sell

   2nd Part: out

   Meaning: all the tickets are completely gone; sold in advance

4. 1st Part: short

   2nd Part: coming

   Meaning: all the things wrong with her husband; his faults

5. 1st Part: law

   2nd Part: suit

   Meaning: a law case brought into a court

6. 1st Part: scatter

   2nd Part: brained

   Meaning: can't keep anything on his mind; his thoughts are all over the place

ANSWERS AND EXPLANATIONS—REVIEW EXERCISES

Review Exercise 1

1. happiness
2. mindless or mindful
3. harmful or harmless
4. sweetness
5. powerful or powerless
6. business
7. needless
8. joyful or joyless
9. careful or careless
10. beautiful

Review Exercise 2

1. superman
2. overcook
3. semidry
4. overpaid
5. semisweet
6. superpower or overpower
7. overbearing
8. supermarket
9. semicircle
10. overdone
11. semifinal
12. superstar
13. overland
14. supernatural
15. overnight

Review Exercise 3

1. flashlight or flashback
2. workshop or workout
3. fullback
4. fishnet
5. blackout
6. fireplace or firelight
7. overcome or overcoat
8. motorcycle
9. outcome
10. loophole

Review Exercise 4

1. sunset
2. hairpin
3. loudmouth
4. warehouse
5. headline

4 | MAKING INFERENCES

WHAT ARE INFERENCES?

Inference is just a big word that means a conclusion or judgment. If you infer that something has happened, you do not see, hear, feel, smell or taste the actual event. But from what you do know, it makes sense to think that it has happened. You make inferences everyday. Most of the time you do so without thinking about it. Suppose you are sitting in front of your house. You hear screeching tires, then a loud crash and breaking glass. You see <u>nothing</u>, but you **infer** that there has been a car accident. We all know the sounds of screeching tires and a crash. We know that these sounds almost always mean a car accident. But there could be some other reason for the sounds. Perhaps it was not an accident. Maybe an angry driver rammed another car. Or maybe someone played the sound of a crash on a record. Or maybe you're hearing things. Making inferences means choosing the <u>most</u> <u>likely</u> explanation for the facts you know.

Look, now, at this drawing. Study all that you see happening.

Imagine that this drawing is a picture of a real event. Now write four facts (**not** inferences) about this picture.

Fact 1:_____

_____

Fact 2:_____

_____

Fact 3:_____

_____

Fact 4:_____

_____

Here are four facts you could have listed:
1. The building has a Pool Hall sign in the window.
2. A man is holding the door of the building open.
3. Another man is outside the building.
4. A pole of some kind is near the building.

If you said something about the man stumbling toward the pole, that's an inference, not a fact. Maybe you thought one fellow was drunk. That may be true, but it's strictly an inference. If you figured the man in the doorway was throwing the other man out—another inference. If you thought the two men had been fighting—another inference.

None of these inferences is wrong for sure. They all could be very true. The important thing to remember is that they are <u>inferences</u>. They are not facts.

You may infer one thing about this drawing and another person may infer something else.

Now tell what you <u>do</u> <u>think</u> took place. What is your inference about this picture? In other words, what do you think has happened? Write your inference here:

_____

_____

_____

_____

You might want to talk about your inference with someone else who has just looked at the drawing. How close are you to making the same inference?

Now try to put yourself in someone else's place. What might a police officer infer if he or she saw this scene? Would that inference be different from yours? Write what you think the police would infer from the scene.

_____

_____

_____

_____

Now put yourself in the place of a 70-year-old lady. What inference might she make when she sees this picture? Write what you think her inference might be.

_____

_____

_____

_____

Now read this short story. Eight sentences follow it. Decide if each sentence is true, false or not known for sure. In the blank in front of the sentence write either true, false or not sure. Remember to be very careful about making inferences. You may look back at the story if you want to.

It was nearly quitting time at the Midwest Tool and Die Company. Mr. Maxwell, the owner, discovered that $1,000 worth of tools was missing.

Besides Mr. Maxwell, four people work at MTD. All of them there knew where these tools were stored. Joe Ware, one worker, had been suspected of a theft six months ago. But, at the time, there were no facts to prove it. So no charges were placed against him.

Mr. Maxwell called his insurance company. Then he told everyone not to leave the shop.

_____1.   The tools were stolen from the Midwest Tool and Die Company.

_____2.   The robbery was discovered at 4:45 P.M.

_____3.   Mr. Maxwell, the owner, found that the tools were missing.

_____4.   Five people worked at the Midwest Tool and Die Company.

_____5.   Joe Ware was thought to have taken the tools.

_____6.   Mr. Maxwell made everyone stay after quitting time.

_____7. The insurance company was coming to question everyone.

_____8. Joe Ware had been arrested for theft before.

The answer to number one would have to be not sure. The tools are missing, but they may not have been stolen. Number two is also not sure. We don't know if it was a robbery or not. We also don't know if the tools were missing right at 4:45 P.M. Number three is true. Mr. Maxwell did find the tools missing. The fourth sentence is also true. But number five is not sure. Joe Ware had been suspected before, but the story says nothing about *this* time. Six is a true statement. Number seven is not sure. We don't know what the insurance company will do. All we know is that Mr. Maxwell called them. The last one is false. Joe had been suspected before but not arrested. There wasn't enough evidence.

Now read and do the following exercises on inferences.

Exercise 1

Read the story below. After the story you will find eight statements. Write true in front of the statements that are facts. Write false in front of those that are not facts. On those you can't tell for sure, write not sure.

John Frame worked at The Soho Bar and Grill. He usually left work at 2:00 A.M. and walked the four blocks to the Blackstone Apartments, where he lived. At 2:00 A.M. the streets were usually quiet.

The past two nights John had been nervous. As he walked home he had heard footsteps behind him. He would stop to see where they were coming from and then hurry on. It was a strange feeling. Could some angry, crazy customer from the Soho be after him?

On May 3rd it happened again. John thought he heard footsteps. This time they sounded like someone running. He ran to his apartment steps. There was a flash; a loud noise rang through the warm night. The neighbors found John lying at the bottom of his apartment steps.

_____ 1. John worked six nights a week at The Soho Bar and Grill.

_____ 2. John heard footsteps.

_____ 3. John lived three miles from The Soho Bar and Grill.

_____ 4. Some crazy guy from the bar was after John.

_____ 5. On May 3rd the footsteps sounded as if someone were running.

_____ 6. A shot rang out through the night.

_____ 7. The person following John fired the shot.

_____ 8. John dropped dead in front of the Black-stone Apartments.

Answers start on page 169.

Exercise 2

Read the following story. Then answer the questions after it.

The train engineer saw what looked like a man lying near the railroad track, just in front of the tunnel. He slammed on the brakes. The freight train ground to a screaming stop.

The crew rushed out to where the body was lying. They saw right away that it was not a real man. It looked like a half-man, half-ape creature. It seemed that it had been sleeping by the tracks.

The creature had inch-long shiny black hair all over its body. Only its face, hands and the bottom of its feet were not hairy. The creature looked to be about four and a half feet tall.   It seemed to weigh about 125 pounds.

The train crew got a rope and tied the creature up. They built a cage for it in one of the boxcars. George Tillman, one of the crew, became the creature's keeper. He named it "Jacko." He started taking care of it and found that Jacko's favorite foods were berries and milk.

Then the crew took Jacko to the college in town. No one there knew what kind of creature Jacko was. Some thought he belonged to an unknown species. Others said Jacko was like a young Bigfoot—a human-like creature they had heard about.

Tillman decided to make money by taking Jacko on tour around the U.S. He would put him on show. He grew excited about his money-making plan. But Jacko suddenly disappeared. No one ever saw him again.

1. What inference did the engineer of the train make?
    _____(1)   He thought he saw a creature with shiny hair.
    _____(2)   He thought he had better slow down.
    _____(3)   He thought the crew wanted to stop.
    _____(4)   He thought he saw a man lying by the tracks.
    _____(5)   He thought his brakes would not work.

2. What did the engineer do because of the inference he made?

_____(1)   He slowed down.

_____(2)   He slammed on his brakes.

_____(3)   He took the creature to a college.

_____(4)   He asked the crew what they thought.

_____(5)   He made a cage for the creature.

3. What was the inference the crew made about why the creature was lying by the side of the tracks?

_____(1)   They thought Jacko had been sleeping there.

_____(2)   They thought the creature was going to attack them.

_____(3)   They thought he was looking for food.

_____(4)   They thought he was lonely and looking for friends.

_____(5)   They thought he was afraid and was hiding.

4. Why else might Jacko have been lying by the tracks?

_____(1)   He could have been working for the railroad.

_____(2)   The crew and engineer were just seeing things.

_____(3)   He could have come by boat.

_____(4)   He was a college student from the town.

_____(5)   He could have been hit by another train.

5. Some of the people at the college inferred that Jacko

_____(1)   escaped from a zoo.

_____(2)   was not dangerous.

_____(3)   was Bigfoot.

_____(4)   was not afraid of them.

_____(5)   liked the cage the crew made.

6. What inference might you make about Jacko's disappearance?

_____(1) George Tillman killed him.

_____(2) He could have escaped.

_____(3) He killed himself in the cage.

_____(4) The college decided to send him away.

_____(5) He stepped out for a minute.

Answers start on page 169.

Exercise 3

Read the following short story. Answer the questions that follow it. The questions ask you to make inferences from the facts in the story.

It was a gray Sunday in April. The game was about to start. "Dead Arm" Reilly had just finished his warm-up. He came back to the dugout and said, "Hell, fellows, I'm still cold. Let's start a fire."

"Good idea!" agreed Jack Fork, our catcher.

"Hold it!" yelled Shorty Rollins, the manager. "You clowns can't start a fire around here. You'll burn down the dugout, the bleachers and everything."

"That wouldn't be any loss," said Dead Arm. "This dump should have been burned down years ago."

Dead Arm and Jack trotted out to right field. Out there a tree had fallen through the fence. It was just lying there. The two of them gathered branches. Then they started a fire right in front of the dugout. There were 30 or 40 fans in the bleachers waiting for the game to start. They all began laughing. Shorty Rollins snorted and cursed. But the team let the fire burn on. The whole team was huddled around it warming their hands.

"Play ball!" the umpire called.

"Get out there, you clowns!" screamed Shorty.

Dead Arm grabbed a ball. He held it over the flames. Then he and the rest of the team took their places.

The other team was up. The first two batters struck out. But the third one hit a hard foul straight at our dugout.

The ball plowed into the fire and scattered branches everywhere. Shorty ran from the dugout and stomped on the branches. "I told you clowns," he screamed.

The game stopped, and the teams and fans watched Shorty. They yelled and whistled at him. Shorty stalked back into the dugout and sat on the bench.

Suddenly a scream of pain came from the dugout. Two batboys struggled from the dugout carrying Shorty's limp body between them.

1. "Dead Arm" Reilly is the _____ for this team.
    Write two facts that this inference could be based on:
    (a)_____

    (b)_____

2. Dead Arm Reilly has some _____ ideas.
    Write two facts you used to make your inference.
    (a)_____

    (b)_____

3. Shorty Rollins, the team's manager, has a _____ opinion of some of his players.
    Write two facts you used to make this inference.
    (a)_____

    (b)_____

4. The ball field itself is in _____ condition.
    Write two facts you used to make this inference.
    (a)_____

    (b)_____

5. The team's opinion of Shorty Rollins, their manager, is

    _____.

    Write two facts you used to make this inference.
    (a)_____

    (b)_____

6. In the last paragraph of the story there are two facts.
    What inference would you make about what happened
    to Shorty from these two? Check one of the following.
    _____(1) Shorty could have been getting more wood
               for the fire.
    _____(2) Shorty might have gone home for a nap.
    _____(3) Shorty sat on a hot branch and fell off his
               seat, knocking himself out.
    _____(4) Shorty scored a home run and fainted.
    _____(5) Shorty had been sitting in the stands watch-
               ing the game.

    Answers start on page 170.

Exercise 4

Read the following short story. After the story, read the 20
facts given. In front of each fact that is true, write the word
true. Write <u>false</u> in front of the statements that are false. If
the statement is an inference and not a fact, write <u>not sure</u>.
You may look back at the story.

The police car was cruising only a block from the Quick Stop Grocery Store. A man came running up to it. He jumped from the curb and waved wildly at the police.

"Hey! Hey! There's been a holdup at Quick Stop," the man shouted. "A guy's running down the alley."

The police car burned rubber and wheeled around in the traffic. The lights flashed and the siren screamed. Then the car skidded into the alley.

A man walked down the alley ahead of the police car. He was carrying a brown paper bag. He spun around and stared at the flashing lights. Then he broke into a wild run. He scrambled from one side of the alley to the other.

When the police closed in, the man threw away the bag and stopped. He raised his hands over his head. The police car ground to a halt. The two officers jumped out with their guns drawn.

The man stood, arms over his head. He made grunting noises. He dropped one hand and pointed at his mouth. Suddenly with the other hand, the man reached inside his coat pocket.

A shot rang out. With a horrified look the man grabbed his chest with both hands. Slowly he slumped to the ground.

_____ 1. The police were cruising only one block from the Quick Stop Grocery Store.

_____ 2. Someone who saw the robbery stopped the police.

_____ 3. That person said the robber was running down the alley.

_____ 4. The police turned off their lights and the siren.

_____ 5. The police made a U-turn and sped to the alley.

_____ 6. The police saw a man in the alley carrying a brown paper bag.

_____ 7. Money from the holdup was in the paper bag.

_____ 8. The man started to run.

_____ 9. He ran from side-to-side looking for a way to escape.

_____10. The man hid the paper bag under his coat.

_____11. The police jumped from the car with their guns out.

_____12. Before the police got out of the car, the man had raised his hands.

_____13. One policeman read the man his rights.

_____14. The man made grunting noises because he couldn't talk.

_____15. The man refused to lean against the hood of the police car.

_____16. The man pointed at his mouth with one hand.

_____17. Suddenly the man reached for a gun in his coat pocket.

_____18. One of the police fired a shot.

_____19.   The shot hit the man in the chest.

_____20.   The man fell to the ground.

Answers start on page 171.

MORE ABOUT MAKING INFERENCES

Making inferences is an important skill. We use this skill everyday in our lives. Making good inferences means using facts to say that something is true. It is important to know when inferences are being made and when real facts are being stated. It is important to know the difference between good inferences and bad inferences. Good inferences are based on facts and on likely explanations for the facts.

REVIEW EXERCISES—MAKING INFERENCES

Review Exercise 1

Read the following comments. Then use the facts to make good inferences. Answer the questions that follow.

These were the comments I overheard while I was there:
"Her face is just as rosy as it ever was."
". . . one of the quickest students in her class."
"If her mother were still alive, she would be proud of her bravery."
"All her little classmates are here."
"That must be her father. He's holding himself together well."

"Look, Grace, they dressed her in her favorite white dress."

"So many people here. The whole town has come to show their respect. And so many flowers!"

"This is one of the saddest days of my life."

1. Where were the people who made the comments?

     _____

2. About how old is the person they talked about?

     _____

3. What might have happened?

     _____

Answers start on page 172.

Review Exercise 2

Read this story. Use the facts to make good inferences. Answer the questions.

The laws finally worked in Robert Griffith's favor. He had worked for many years as an employment counselor in a small city. He'd been a good one, too. People from all walks of life respected him for his concern for them. Nearly anyone out of a job could count on him for help. Then his whole life changed.

An accident. Then doctors, hospitals, operations—all with no success. He would never be himself again. He could have gone on working as he had in the past. But the unfortunate thing was that in that city no one could hire him. They wanted to hire him, but he couldn't get into the buildings. He couldn't get into an office. He couldn't even go to the men's room.

Then laws were enacted that made it possible for him to return to work. He found a job in a building where the doors had been widened. There was a wide front door, and a wide door to the office on the first floor. There was a restroom he could use. Though he couldn't walk around, even on crutches, he could work again. For a second time, his whole life changed.

1. What happened that changed Robert's life after his accident?

    _____

    _____

2. Why did that make it impossible for him to get a job?

    _____

    _____

3. What kind of law must have been enacted to allow Robert to get a job?

    _____

    _____

Answers start on page 172.

Review Exercise 3

Read the story and think about the two people and who they are. Then answer the questions that follow. Use the facts to make good inferences.

He sat in the room next to hers thinking about life—the beauty of life, the pain of life. He had seen her when she was first born. Her mother had gone through such pain, and then felt such joy. But her mother didn't even live to see her become three days old.

Now she slept for a while without any sense of anything. Just sleep—mindless sleep—knowing nothing that was going on around her. For days and nights, for weeks, he had kept watch over her. When she would wake up and cry, he would soothe her. He had to think fast and hard about what to do to bring her relief. After all, she couldn't tell him what she was crying for. She hadn't the ability to communicate that. But, because of his love for her, he could usually figure out what he needed to do for her. And then she would go off to sleep again.

Sometimes after she went to sleep, he would stare at her wrinkled face that had grown so thin. He would remember the pleasure of many years of knowing her. And he would wonder with pain why it was that he would probably outlive her.

1. In this story, "she" is probably

    _____(1) a baby.

    _____(2) a young girl.

    _____(3) an older woman.

    _____(4) a teenage girl.

    _____(5) You can't tell from what is given.

2. In this story, "he" could be

    _____(1) her brother.

    _____(2) her father.

    _____(3) her husband.

    _____(4) her doctor.

    _____(5) any of the above

3. Who is older, "he" or "she"?

_____(1) You can't tell from the story.

_____(2) He is older.

_____(3) They are the same age.

_____(4) She is older.

_____(5) It makes no difference.

4. He feels sad that he will probably outlive her. What is the most likely reason he thinks that will happen?

_____

_____

_____

_____

ANSWERS AND EXPLANATIONS—MAKING INFERENCES

Exercise 1

1. Not sure. We don't know how many nights a week John worked.
2. True. John did hear footsteps.
3. False. John lived only four blocks from the bar.
4. Not sure. John didn't know for sure that the footsteps were those of someone from The Soho.
5. True. John thought the footsteps sounded like someone was running.
6. Not sure. There was a noise and a flash of light. We don't know that these were caused by a gunshot.
7. Not sure. We don't know that there was a gunshot.
8. Not sure. Again, we don't really know why John is lying there. We don't even know if he's dead. He might have fallen.

Exercise 2

1. (4) The engineer thought a man was lying by the tracks.
2. (2) He slammed on his brakes because of his inference.
3. (1) The crew thought Jacko had been sleeping there.
4. (5) Other things could have happened to explain why Jacko was lying there. He could have fallen and been knocked unconscious. Another train might have hit him, or he might have been very tired.
5. (3) They inferred that he could be Bigfoot because they stated he was like a young Bigfoot. This was based on what they had heard about such a creature.

6. (2) He could have escaped from Tillman; Tillman could
     have let him go; someone could have stolen him or
     many other things could have taken place. We don't
     know for sure. (2) makes the most sense.

Exercise 3

1. pitcher
    (a) His nickname is "Dead Arm."
    (b) He was the one who took the heated ball to the field.
2. strange, odd, different, funny (You may have used other
    words.)
    (a) He wanted to start a fire in front of the dugout.
    (b) He heated the ball over the fire; or, he went to right
        field to gather firewood.
3. poor, low, not very good, terrible (You may have used
    other words.)
    (a) He calls the players "clowns."
    (b) He wouldn't go along with building the fire. He
        ordered them out on the field, like a bunch of kids.
4. bad, poor, terrible or some word like these.
    (a) The field was so old anything could start it on fire.
    (b) A tree fell through the right-field fence and was still
        there. Dead Arm called the whole park a dump.
5. not very high, poor or some word like these.
    (a) They paid no attention to him and built the fire
        anyway.
    (b) They stopped the game and laughed and yelled at
        Shorty as he tried to put out the fire.
6. (3) Shorty might have sat on a hot branch. He could
     have fallen off the bench and knocked himself out.
     (You may have some other inference just as good as
     this one.) But none of the other choices fits the
     facts: There was a scream of pain and Shorty was
     carried out of the dugout.

Exercise 4

1. True; we are given this fact in the first sentence.
2. Not sure; all we know is that a man stopped the police. He told them there had been a holdup. We don't know if he saw it. We don't even know if there really <u>was</u> a robbery at the store.
3. Not sure; all the man said was that <u>a guy</u> was running down the alley.
4. False; they turned <u>on</u> their lights and the siren.
5. Not sure; we don't know what kind of turn they made.
6. True
7. Not sure; we never find out what the man had in the bag.
8. True
9. Not sure; we don't really know that the man was trying to escape.
10. False; the man threw the bag away.
11. True
12. True
13. False; we are never told that this was done.
14. Not sure; the man made noises, but we don't know why.
15. False; we are never told that this happened.
16. True
17. Not sure; we only know that the man reached inside his coat pocket. We don't know what he was going to pull out.
18. Not sure; a shot rang out, but we are not told where it came from.
19. Not sure; the man grabbed his chest, but we don't know if he had been shot.
20. True

ANSWERS AND EXPLANATIONS—REVIEW EXERCISES

Review Exercise 1

1. They were at a funeral, or in a funeral parlor.
2. Rather young. Probably school-age. This is true because one person says, "All her <u>little</u> classmates are here."
3. The young girl must have died while doing an act of bravery. Or, the young girl was very brave during a disease that finally killed her.

Review Exercise 2

1. He was unable to work. He could not use a cane. He had to use a wheelchair.
2. The wheelchair was too wide to go through the doors of offices.
3. The law must have forced companies to widen their doors and make other changes so that handicapped people could work there.

Review Exercise 3

1. (3) an older woman; she is wrinkled. Also, the man had known her for many years. The beginning of

the story makes you think the story is about a baby.

2. (5) any of the above; whoever "he" is, he saw her just after she was born. Any of the four men mentioned could be older than she and could have seen her just after she was born.

3. (2) He is older; he saw her just after she was born.

4. He doesn't think he is going to die soon, but he does think she is going to die soon. She is probably very ill.

POST-TEST

Directions: You will be using all of the reading skills you worked on in this book to answer the 38 questions on the Post-Test. Follow the directions given.

When you have finished the Post-Test, check your answers in the section that follows, beginning on page 184. Then fill in the Skill Mastery Chart on page 187. By comparing your scores on the Pre-Test and Post-Test you can see how much you've learned.

If you get a low final score on any of the tested reading skills, review those units of the book.

Read the following passage.

For centuries people all over the world have feared lightning. They have believed all kinds of strange things about it.

Some people in earlier times thought lightning was their gods having a war among themselves. Others believed the gods were angry with human beings. Still others felt that the devil caused the lightning.

Just 50 years ago two scientists studied lightning seriously. They wanted to discover the exact nature of lightning.

They found that lightning is not just one single huge bolt. It is a series of sparks or shots. These shots hit one place very fast.

First, lightning sends out a downward series of shots or sparks from a cloud. This is invisible. In one-millionth of a second this first series of shots makes a path for the next series. The second series goes from the ground back to the cloud. Its speed makes it invisible too.

Next, the path to the ground is filled with a steady current of electricity. This current is called "hot" lightning. We now can see and hear it. Its heat causes air to expand and make thunder. Hot lightning destroys whatever it hits.

Some people think that lightning never strikes twice in the same place. This is wrong. Big buildings like the Empire State Building in New York have been hit hundreds of times.

Even smaller buildings get hit more than once. In Michigan lightning started a fire in a barn. While a crowd watched the fire, two more lightning bolts struck the barn.

Lightning can do strange things, too. It has melted metal objects like jewelry and zippers on clothes. The person wearing these was not hurt.

But many people have been killed instantly by lightning. People have always feared lightning. There is good reason for that fear.

Put a check mark in front of the best ending for each statement.

1. Some people living long ago believed that lightning
   _____(1)   was the war of God and the devil.
   _____(2)   was the gods having a party.
   _____(3)   was the devil trying to destroy human beings.
   _____(4)   was the gods who were angry with human beings.
   _____(5)   all of the above

2. Serious study of lightning started just
   _____(1)   20 years ago.
   _____(2)   50 years ago.
   _____(3)   40 years ago.
   _____(4)   30 years ago.
   _____(5)   none of the above

3. Lightning really is
   _____(1) one huge bolt.
   _____(2) two huge bolts.
   _____(3) a series of shots.
   _____(4) one shot down and one shot back.
   _____(5) none of the above

4. "Hot" lightning is what
   _____(1) melts through everything it touches.
   _____(2) we see and hear.
   _____(3) we call the second bolt.
   _____(4) we call the third bolt.
   _____(5) all of the above

5. Thunder then is caused by
   _____(1) the angry gods.
   _____(2) the angry devil.
   _____(3) heat and expanding air.
   _____(4) the crash of whatever it hits.
   _____(5) none of the above

6. Some people think that
   _____(1) lightning never strikes twice in the same
                spot.
   _____(2) lightning has many superstitions connected
                with it.
   _____(3) only chain lightning is really dangerous.
   _____(4) lightning will always be a mystery to us.
   _____(5) all of the above

7. A barn fire in Michigan proved that

_____(1) all crowds draw lightning quickly.

_____(2) you should never watch a fire in a thunderstorm.

_____(3) people like to watch any kind of fire in any weather.

_____(4) one old idea about lightning striking is wrong.

_____(5) all of the above

8. A melted zipper on a man's pants shows

_____(1) that lightning can do odd things.

_____(2) that lightning is nothing to fear.

_____(3) that lightning is always attracted to metal.

_____(4) that it's best to wear plastic zippers in a thunderstorm.

_____(5) none of the above

9. The main idea of this article is

_____(1) that lightning is now understood and need not be considered dangerous.

_____(2) that two scientists were able to destroy many superstitions about lightning.

_____(3) that more knowledge about lightning gives us good reason to be cautious about it.

_____(4) that more people than not are killed by lightning.

_____(5) none of the above

_____

On the following page choose the one word from each column to make a compound word. Do not use any word more than once. Write your words in the blanks that are after the lists. (When you check your answers and add up your score, give yourself ½ a point for each correct answer.)

10. man   fold   10. _____

11. chain   room   11. _____

12. broad   cast   12. _____

13. head   slinger   13. _____

14. center   quarters   14. _____

15. gun   stream   15. _____

16. main   going   16. _____

17. space   hole   17. _____

18. wash   smoker   18. _____

19. on   craft   19. _____

Read this story.

The Titanic was the largest and fanciest steamship ever put to sea. It weighed over 45,000 tons and was more than 800 feet long. The owners of the Titanic claimed that it was unsinkable. Neither storms, high waves or even icebergs could hurt it.

In April of 1912 the Titantic sailed from Southhampton, England for New York City. More than 2,000 people were on board.

As the ship sailed through the North Atlantic Ocean, it received many warning messages. These were about dangerous icebergs in the area. The warnings went unheeded. Didn't the owners claim that the ship was unsinkable?

On April 14, 1912 the Titanic steamed into the middle of the iceberg area. The ship was traveling at a speed of 40 miles an hour. The captain wanted to arrive in New York City early.

Shortly before midnight the ship slammed into an iceberg. The damage done to the "unsinkable" ship made it certain that it would go down. Yet the crew didn't tell the passengers about this right away.

Finally, the crew began firing distress rockets and sending out emergency radio calls.

A ship named the Californian was less than ten miles from the Titanic. It saw the rockets and heard the radio signals, but paid no attention.

Another ship, the Carpathia, was farther away. But it turned around and came back to pick up survivors.

The Titanic's passengers and crew started getting into the lifeboats. There weren't enough boats for all. To make matters worse, some boats left less than half full.

Two hours and 40 minutes after the collision with the iceberg, the Titanic sank into the icy water. About 1,500 people went down with the ship. It was one of the great tragedies in the history of the sea.

Read the following list of events from the story. They have been jumbled. Arrange them in their correct order by writing "1" for the first, "2" for the second, and so on. Do this in the blanks in front of each sentence.

20. _____ The Titanic sinks under the waters of the North Atlantic.

21. _____ The crew starts firing rockets and sending out radio signals.

22. _____ The Titanic receives warnings of icebergs.
23. _____ The Titanic sails from Southhampton, England.
24. _____ The captain speeds up to make New York City early.
25. _____ The ship named Carpathia turns back to help the Titanic.
26. _____ The lifeboats are lowered into the water.
27. _____ The Titanic strikes an iceberg.
28. _____ The ship named the Californian pays no attention to the calls for help.
29. _____ About 1,500 people perish in the "unsink-able" ship.

In each paragraph there is an underlined word or words. Figure out the meaning of the word(s) from the context. Write your answer in the blank after the paragraph.

30. One cigarette company has ads that show their ciga-rettes protruding very far from the smoker's mouth. Almost every ad shows a smoker with a bent cigarette. The smoker has forgotten how far the cigarette pro-trudes. So it has gotten bent at the end.

    protrudes: _____

31. Jim's two friends pulled him from the bottom of the swimming pool. He'd been there for more than five minutes. The lifeguards used mouth-to-mouth breath-ing on Jim for ten minutes. Then the fireman worked on him for an hour. All their efforts were in vain. Jim was dead.

    in vain: _____

32. We saw Red's picture on a poster down at the post office. In fact, there were two pictures of Red right under the big word, WANTED. One picture showed a front view of Red's face. The other was a profile. From the profile we could see how big Red's nose was.

profile: _____

_____

Read the following short story.

My grandmother was always a very strong woman. Even now. She has had a stroke. She can't talk and can barely move.

When we were little, she was very strict with us. She said things only once: "Time for bed, children." If we didn't move, her eyes would look straight at us and start blinking evenly. One, two, three, four. She seemed to stop breathing. The blinking would get faster. The faster she blinked, the faster we'd better move. I never found out what would happen if I didn't go. I was always too afraid to wait around to see.

I think the lesson behind her strictness was, "You have to do what you have to do." She was there to tell us what "have to" meant. She showed us that doing "what you have to" with cheer made it easier.

I thought about that last Christmas. She sat with her children, grandchildren and great grandchildren all around her. She was enjoying herself. But, because she needs a lot of rest, my mother said to her, "Time for bed, Mother."

Those same eyes that used to blink at us looked at mother. They seemed to say, "Do I have to?" Then they looked at me smilingly, saying, "If I must, I must. You know how it is." She pulled herself up on her cane. She winked at me, smiled and began the slow and painful journey to her bedroom.

Put a check mark next to the best answer for each of the three questions.

33. The grandmother in this reading had a stroke
    _____(1) when the writer was a child.
    _____(2) before the Christmas that was mentioned.
    _____(3) after the Christmas that was mentioned.
    _____(4) when the writer was a teenager.
    _____(5) It is not possible to tell.

34. The grandmother told her grandchildren what to do. If they didn't do it, she would
    _____(1) just look at them, seeming to say, "You must."
    _____(2) repeat what she said in a louder voice.
    _____(3) blink her eyes.
    _____(4) stop breathing. She wanted them to think she would die if they didn't obey.
    _____(5) spank them.

35. In the last paragraph the grandmother says a lot with her eyes. Why didn't she just talk?
    _____(1) She couldn't talk.
    _____(2) She didn't want to wake the children.
    _____(3) She was always the strong, silent type.
    _____(4) She was angry about having to go to bed.
    _____(5) She was afraid of what she might say if she talked.

Read this story. Then answer the questions that follow. Use the facts to make good inferences.

George lived alone in his first apartment. He had finally managed to scrape together enough money to get a place of his own. It wasn't much, but he took pride in the fact that it was all his.

George felt his life was finally coming together. He had gotten a job with a real future. The company was going to pay for him to go to school while he worked. He was slowly beginning to buy the things he wanted for his "bachelor pad." He felt proud of himself for making it on his own at his age.

One winter morning George awoke and went to put on some music. He enjoyed his new stereo and needed that music to get him going in the morning. But that morning, he got going in a flash—and with no music—when he saw what had happened. What jolted him awake was the cold air blowing through the window—the same window he had closed the night before. As he looked around his empty apartment the truth sunk in. There would be no more music for George.

36. What probably happened that night at George's apartment?

_____

_____

37. About how old is George?

_____

38. Which sentence do you think is true about George?

_____(1)   He is dependent upon everyone but himself.

_____(2)   George is the sort of person who likes to make it on his own.

_____(3)   George has fits of anger.

_____(4)   George is very easy-going and would rather listen to music than anything else.

_____(5)   You can't tell anything about George from this passage.

ANSWERS AND EXPLANATIONS— POST-TEST

1. (4) The passage says that some people thought lightning happened when the gods were angry with people. Others thought it was because their gods were having a war among themselves. Still others felt that the devil caused lightning.

2. (2) 50 years ago. This detail is found in the third paragraph.

3. (3) a series of shots. This detail is found in the fourth and fifth paragraphs.

4. (2) we see and hear. This detail is found in the sixth paragraph.

5. (3) heat and expanding air. This detail is also found in the sixth paragraph.

6. (1) lightning never strikes twice in the same spot. This statement begins the seventh paragraph.

7. (4) one old idea about lightning is wrong. The Michigan fire is described in the eighth paragraph. The same barn was hit by lightning three times.

8. (1) that lightning can do odd things. The ninth paragraph tells that zippers on clothes can be melted by lightning without hurting the person.

9. (3) that more knowledge about lightning gives us good reason to be cautious about it. The last paragraph sums up the main idea of the passage.

These are the words you should have made: Give yourself ½ a point for each right answer.

10. manhole
11. chainsmoker
12. broadcast
13. headquarters
14. centerfold

15. gunslinger
16. mainstream
17. spacecraft
18. washroom
19. ongoing

20.	(9)	25.	(7)
21.	(5)	26.	(8)
22.	(2)	27.	(4)
23.	(1)	28.	(6)
24.	(3)	29.	(10)

Your answers don't have to be exactly what is written here, so long as they have the same idea.

30. protrudes: sticks out; juts out. You can figure out the meaning of protrudes by the description of what happened to the cigarettes.

31. in vain: useless; didn't do any good. You can figure out that the rescue attempts did not work because Jim died.

32. profile: side view. You can figure out that profile means a side view by the fact that there were

33. (2) You can tell that the grandmother has already had a stroke at the time the story takes place.

34. (3) This is mentioned in the second paragraph. The grandmother would blink her eyes.

35. (1) We were told at the beginning of the story that the grandmother was not able to talk after the stroke.

36. It seems that someone broke in and robbed him. His stereo was gone.

37. He is probably in his late teens or early 20s. He felt proud making it on his own at his age.

38. (2) He was proud to make it on his own.
The other choices are wrong. (1) He is not dependent on anyone. (3) There is no evidence that he has fits of anger. (4) George listens to music to get himself awake. But he is hard-working: he has a job and goes to school at the same time. He is not easy-going. (5) You <u>can</u> infer some things about George from the story.

POST-TEST SKILL MASTERY CHART

Directions: Fill in the Skill Mastery Chart after you have checked your work on the Post-Test. Each skill on the test is listed with the test questions using that skill. Circle each question you answered correctly. Then count your total number of circled answers and write this in the box under Number Correct. Next, find the Skill Mastery Level that fits your number correct. Place a check (✔) in the box at the right level. Do this for each skill listed. Then find your total number of correct answers and total number of checks at each Skill Mastery Level. Compare your results on the Post-Test with what you did on the Pre-Test Skill Mastery Chart. Both charts will show you what your next step should be in building your reading skills.

SKILL	TOTAL SCORE	NUMBER CORRECT	SKILL MASTERY LEVELS			STUDY PAGES
			SKILL MASTERY	PRACTICE & REVIEW NEEDED	FULL LEARNING NEEDED	
			(Check one box in each row.)			
1 Seeing the Main Idea and Supporting Details 1, 2, 3, 4, 5 6, 7, 8, 9 33, 34, 35	12		12-9	8-5	4-0	17-75
2 How Details Are Arranged 20, 21, 22, 23, 24 25, 26, 27, 28, 29	10		10-8	7-5	4-0	76-122
3 Learning New Words When Reading (10, 11, 12, 13, 14)* (15, 16, 17, 18, 19)* 30, 31, 32	8		8-7	6-4	3-0	123-150
4 Making Inferences 36, 37, 38	3		3-2	1	0	151-173
TOTAL	33					

Each question is worth one-half point.